FROM THE PILOT FACTORY, 1942

William P. Mitchell

Texas A&M University Press
College Station

The paper used in this book meets the minimum requirements
of the American National Standard for Permanence
of Paper for Printed Library Materials, z39.48-1984.
Binding materials have been chosen for durability.
⊗

Library of Congress Cataloging-in-Publication Data

Mitchell, William, 1922–
    From the pilot factory, 1942 / William P. Mitchell.—1st ed.
        p. cm. — (Centennial of flight series ; no. 14)
    Includes bibliographical references and index.
    ISBN 1-58544-387-5 (cloth : alk. paper)
    1. Mitchell, William, 1922—Correspondence.   2. World War,
1939–1945—Aerial operations, American.   3. World War,
1939–1945—Personal narratives, American.   4. World War,
1939–1945—Campaigns—Western Front.   5. Air pilots, Military—
Training of—United States—History—20th century.   6. Air pilots,
Military—United States—Correspondence.   7. United States, Army
Air Forces—Officers—Correspondence.   I. Title.   II. Series.
    D790.M558 2005
    940.54′4973′092—dc22

                                                    2004014462

For my children, Kate, Brooks, Ann, Liz, and Spencer, who grew up hearing me tell bits and pieces of this story; for my mother, who faithfully replied to my letters, and who saved and boxed every one of them; and for Marian Mitchell, who took over custody of the letters, which have now survived for more than sixty years.

CONTENTS

PREFACE

U ntil 1939, pilot training in the U.S. Army Air Force was highly individualized. The program produced skillful pilots and highly qualified junior officers. But only about twelve hundred pilots were graduated in 1939. In 1940 the annual pilot-production goal was raised twice: first to seven thousand graduates per year, then to twelve thousand. In 1941 the goal was raised to thirty thousand, and by 1942–43 the goal was set at fifty thousand graduate pilots per year, where it peaked. As air force historian Rebecca Cameron explains in her book *Training to Fly: Military Flight Training, 1917–1945,* the training methodology changed from piecework to mass production. The academy became a factory.

I was accepted as an aviation cadet in Class 42-J. I entered the program in March, 1942. I expected memories of those months to last indefinitely. But as the years passed, flight school became just a dim blur of scenes. I could remember a few faces, buildings, and airplanes. But events? Emotions? Relationships? I could not even remember my first solo flight.

Then a box of letters turned up in 2001. In it were my letters. I had started writing home when I was a nineteen-year-old cadet. I kept writing throughout the war, but censorship, later on, made it impossible to describe what was going on.

The best letters are the first ones, the ones from flight school. My mother saved them all. She kept the letters in the order in which they arrived. And they arrived, on average, about twice a week. Altogether, they provide a chronological record of one cadet's experiences as he was first processed through the pilot factory in 1942, and then moved along to a World War II operational theater.

Jim Sadkovich was the first to evaluate the letters I thought might be the makings of a book. At the time, Jim was an acquisitions editor at Texas A&M University Press. He and the readers he asked to judge my proposal gave me the encouragement and direction I needed to proceed with the manuscript. Thank you, Jim.

Guidance in preparing the manuscript for production was provided by Stephanie George, assistant managing editor at Texas A&M University Press. Thank you for your patience, Stephanie.

Help in cross-checking some names and events came from former 73d Squadron buddies. They include Bill Brown, John Devitt, Bill Chaple, Hugh Gunn, Fred Jones, and Boris Shvetzoff. The manuscript was formatted and put on a disk by Mark Gabel and Adriana van Stralen of Chapel Hill, North Carolina. Source material was provided by the following individuals and institutions: Bruce Ashcroft, historian at the AETCO/HO at Randolph Air Force Base, Texas; Jim Kitchens III from the Office of Historical Research at the Air University, Maxwell Field, Alabama; Lucy Sandoval from the El Progreso Library in Uvalde, Texas; Leroy Walter at the Aviation History Museum in Uvalde, Texas; Rose Watkins and Becky Thomas from the Knight Museum in Alliance, Nebraska; and the staff of the photo library at the University of Texas Institute of Texan Cultures in San Antonio, Texas.

A special thank you goes to Marion Davies, who advised me to junk a long-winded introduction and get right to the letters.

Another special thank you goes to my stepdaughter Claire McKean, an editor in New York City, who devoted a long weekend to helping me nitpick the page proofs of this book.

FROM THE PILOT FACTORY, 1942

A GOOD DAY AT THE FACTORY

I t is a Thursday night in early May, 1942. I am an aviation cadet in the Army Air Corps' pilot-training program. I am writing to my parents from Garner Field in Uvalde, Texas. It is one of many new primary flying schools established by the air corps. I am poised to make my first solo flight.

Dear Folks,

I really got a workout today—an hour and three minutes of takeoffs, landings, stalls, spins, and one slow roll, which was done by my instructor. It boosted my time to seven hours and eight minutes, and I should solo Saturday, providing everything works out OK.

I did five landings today, and three of them were of the grasshopper variety—three skips and a jump. When we're shooting landings like we did today, we do what is known as racehorse landings. We come in, touch our wheels to the ground, then gun the throttle and take right off again. We have landing flaps on our wings to slow our speed down when we come in to land, and we just use half flaps, unless it's a forced landing in a very small field. As soon as we land, we are sup-posed to raise the flaps again, because the plane is harder to handle with the flaps down. We were in the midst of a racehorse landing, and were taking off. My instructor told me to raise the flaps, and for some dumb reason, I lowered them to full flaps. Boy, the plane kind of waltzed around, and I really fixed those flaps in a big hurry. I just sat there then and waited for the instructor to start bawling me out good and proper, but he just sat there and laughed. He said that he should've told me off but it was so darned funny that he just couldn't.

There was a strong wind blowing this afternoon, and it was almost impossible to make a smooth landing.

We went up to five thousand today for spins and stalls. We were about a thousand feet above the clouds and it sure was beautiful, and the air was just as smooth as silk. My instructor really felt good today, and we played around a little bit. We were following the main highway, and we'd zoom down at cars and wiggle our wings at buses—it sure was a lot of fun.

I'm beginning to get the feel of the plane now, and it's beginning to feel like my old Victory Six [a 1926 Dodge coupe I drove to work].

I guess you've noticed that in all my letters all I talk about is flying. That's not all we do, by any means, but it's all I can think about, and I'm really crazy about it. We have ground school, athletics, drill, inspections, and Saturday nights and Sundays off, but I don't give a hoot about any of them. I just can't keep my mind off flying.

General Marshall, chief of staff of the U.S. Army, will be here tomorrow, so I'd better buckle down and clean this place up.

Love to all,
Billy

A BAD DAY

Two days have passed since the last letter.

Dear Folks,

Well, the whole situation has changed now, and I'm down low in the dumps. Saturday, when I was all set to solo, I went up and flew worse than I ever have before, and instead of soloing, I came awful close to getting an elimination ride. I did everything wrong, and I don't know why—I guess I was just too keyed up. After we got down, my instructor sat down and looked at me and said, "Mitchell, what on earth happened to you? Are you sick? You sure did let me down!"

Then he said, "The way you flew today would give me every right in the world to put you up for elimination, and if I didn't think you could do it, I'd wash you right now, but I really think you can fly, so Monday I want you to show me!" That made me feel a little better, but I'm still worried.

Three days, Thursday, Friday, Saturday, saw about a quarter of our bunch get put up for elimination; it was really bad. Murphy got it, and that just about kills me.

Tomorrow might tell the tale—I'll either solo or make a darned good showing—otherwise I'm up for elimination. None of the fellows in my group has soloed, and two of them are already eliminated.

I think I'll do all right, because I know that I can fly all right—I just had a bad day Saturday, so I should solo Monday.

I played five sets of tennis today with Murphy, and we really had a swell time. I sure hope he can pass his elimination ride, because I'll hate to see him leave.

As soon as I solo, I'll send you a telegram so that you will know that everything is OK.

I have to study now. Write as often as you can.

Love to all,
Billy

HOW THE PILOT FACTORY CAME TO BE

Americans who were tuned to the radio during the Battle of Britain knew that air power had added a new dimension to warfare. Few Americans, though, grasped the magnitude of what had happened—that control of the air was now essential to victory in virtually any military engagement. Fewer still were aware that the United States did not possess a modern air arm of its own.

The seriousness of the situation was spelled out in August, 1940, by Secretary of War Henry Stimson. He was testifying before a joint congressional committee.[1]

"Air power today has decided the fate of nations," Stimson said. "Germany with her powerful air armadas has vanquished one people after another. On the ground, large armies have been mobilized to resist her, but each time it was that additional power in the air that decided the fate of each individual nation."

"We are starting late in the game," Stimson warned. "The crisis we need to prepare for is already here," he said. "The time factor is our principal obstacle."

Indeed, time had begun to run out four years earlier. Hermann Göring had put German flying training on a war footing in 1936.[2] The National Socialist Flying Corps encouraged German youth as young as eight to get involved in building model airplanes and gliders. At fourteen the youths could begin to fly sport gliders. At eighteen the student was eligible to enter a Luftwaffe (German air force) training school. But before he could begin actual flight schooling, the pilot candidate had to undergo six months of infantry training. This added the physical toughening and discipline that the high command thought necessary.

By 1939 German air force training had reached a degree of quality not exceeded by any other European air force.[3] The student pilot first underwent a six- to twelve-month course in military discipline. (This phase of training was reduced to two to three months after hostilities began.) Next came the "Flying Training Posting Pool" and two months' instruction in aeronautical subjects. This was followed by "Elementary Flying Training School," where the student got 100 to 150 hours in light planes, and where he was evaluated to determine the type of aircraft for which he was suited.

Bomber and reconnaissance candidates then went to twin-engine school, which was followed by an intensive fifty-hour course in instrument flying. Fighter candidates went to single-engine school where they concentrated on tactics and transition to more advanced aircraft. Finally there was transition training in operational aircraft, and assignment to operational units. Completion of the entire training program required eighteen months to two years and involved about 250 hours of flying.

By 1939, some seventy-five to one hundred flying schools in Germany were turning out ten to fifteen thousand pilots a year. The Luftwaffe had more practical experience in modern flying than any other air force, except, perhaps, Japan's.[4]

The training of pilots in Japan paralleled that of German trainees. Candidates for the Imperial Japanese Navy Air Force started the training program as early as age fifteen. These youths were given up to three years of general education before even beginning basic pilot training. After as much as one year in basic training, they were moved up to advanced training in operational aircraft.[5]

Tacticians and pilots in both Germany and Japan had the advantage of having experienced actual combat prior to their engagement in World War II. Germans got their experience in the Spanish Civil War, where the Luftwaffe's Condor Legion supported the forces of General Franco.[6] Generalmajor Hugo Sperrle, who commanded the Condor operations, rotated key German pilot officers in and out of Spain, allowing as many as possible to taste combat and contribute tactical ideas. German use of aircraft in close support of ground troops—the tactic that made blitzkrieg possible—was a concept that the Condor Legion developed in Spain.

Meanwhile, in the Far East, the Marco Polo Bridge Incident near Peking, in which Japanese troops attacked a Chinese garrison, initiated the conflict between Japan and China in 1937. Japanese naval aircraft operated against China for the next two and a half years. Raids, each involving as many as fifty aircraft, were directed against Canton, Nanchang, Nanking, Hangkow, and other cities. These operations produced seasoned combat pilots, mature fighting men. Of the 350 aircraft that attacked the U.S. base at Pearl Harbor in 1941 (78 fighters, 129 carrier-bombers, and 143 carrier-attack planes), many were flown by veterans of the China conflict.[7] Commander Tadashi Kaneko, for example, had been a fighter pilot for six years at the time of the Pearl Harbor attack. He went on to fight in the Battle of Midway and over Guadalcanal in the Solomon Islands and Rabaul in New Guinea before he was killed in action in November, 1942.[8]

When Secretary Stimson testified about the importance of air power, Nazi forces had just finished crushing Poland, Norway, Belgium, and France. The campaigns required just ten months to complete. At Dunkirk, the British had been fortunate to evacuate what was left of their army on the continent. Nazi bombers were now over England day and night.

"Blitzkrieg" had become a household word in the United States. The term means "lightning war," and it was used in German propaganda to produce a fear of the Luftwaffe.[9] Blitzkrieg was symbolized by tanks and armored personnel carriers in newsreel footage U.S. audiences saw. But it took air power to make blitzkrieg work.

At U.S. military analysts' urging, expansion of the U.S. air arm began in 1939. As the military situation in Europe worsened, the United States allocated more and more funds to building strength in the air. A gigantic program emerged in which the managers, both military and civilian, scrambled to meet deadlines for a broad range of projects. It was a high-stakes game of catch-up.

Paramount, of course, was the design and production of new aircraft. Also, hundreds of new airfields had to be sited and constructed. Maintenance and supply depots were needed. Personnel to crew and maintain the aircraft had to be recruited and trained, and instructors qualified to teach air and ground crews had to be found.

The air corps' pilot training program, as of 1939, was turning out about a thousand graduates a year. That was a drop in the bucket in view of the looming crisis. The production of pilots had to be accelerated tremendously, and the speedup had to begin immediately. The Office of Air Force History likened the situation of the pilot school to that of a medium-sized college graduating three hundred students a year. In the analogy, the college is asked to increase the number of graduates from three hundred to fifty thousand a year. And the increase is to be achieved in three years.[10] That was the scope of the challenge that the air corps took on.

Before 1939, three small classes were inducted into the flying cadet program every year. Students moved through primary, basic, and advanced training at a speed more or less commensurate with the student's ability. After a year of "academy" instruction, the fledgling pilots were commissioned and assigned to tactical units for further training. This program produced skillful pilots and highly qualified junior officers. But relatively few students graduated.

Ultimately, to graduate fifty thousand students a year, the air corps had to modify its emphasis on the individual student. To the credit of the training command, important traditions were preserved. Students stayed with one instructor through each phase of flying training (primary, basic, and advanced). And while the time spent in flight school's three phases was cut from twelve to seven months, a student spent almost as much time in the air as before.

Pilot production was accelerated in four ways:

1. *Institution of a "pre-flight" training phase.* In pre-flight, cadets concentrated on ground school, military indoctrination, and physical conditioning. This allowed the air corps to get a big chunk of classroom instruction (and associated weeding out) accomplished before flight training.[11]
2. *Expansion of flight-training facilities by using civilian contractors.* In 1939 the Air Corps contracted with nine civilian flying schools to provide primary flight training to aviation cadets. This was seen as a way to avoid the time and expense of building and staffing airfields from scratch. Civilian instructors were taught the basics of disciplined flying at Randolph Field, the gold standard of military flying schools. The instructors then went home and applied the Randolph methods at their civilian schools, under the supervision of air corps instructors. The civilian "contract" flying-school concept proved hugely successful. More than fifty such contract schools were participating in pilot training by 1942.[12]
3. *Relaxation of entrance requirements.* Until 1940, pilot candidates had to be twenty years old and have two years of college. By lowering the age minimum to eighteen and eliminating the college requirement, the air corps made pilot training accessible to an as yet untapped pool of young men.[13]
4. *Advertising and publicity.* To make sure their recruiting message got through, the air corps authorized an advertising and publicity campaign. The theme was glamour. The poster boy was a handsome young pilot in helmet, goggles, and white scarf. What turned

out to be a blockbuster in the campaign was the movie *I Wanted Wings,* released in 1940. The movie made an instant star of actress Veronica Lake. It also starred Randolph Field, the air corps' elegant training facility near San Antonio. Randolph became widely known as the "West Point of the Air." The cadets who trained there were seen as the new elite.[14]

The framework for the air corps' pilot factory was in place early in 1942, and production was humming. At some bases there were only tents where there would later be barracks. Lecturers often fought to be heard over the clamor of construction. But pilot graduation quotas were being met. From July 1, 1939, to August 31, 1945, the factory turned out 193,440 air corps pilots.[15]

THE FACTORY DOOR OPENS FOR ME

The air corps would spend $25,000 per student to teach pilot candidates how to fly. Of course, there was no guarantee of graduation. But any young man with good eyes, good health, and a modicum of coordination and intelligence was invited to try.

It looked like a good deal to me—especially after December 7, 1941.

While the Japanese were bombing Pearl Harbor, I was bowling with a friend of mine, Tom Mooney, at an alley near home in Kirkwood, Missouri. When we drove home we found Dad glued to the radio. We listened with him for a while, then Tom and I went to see *Sergeant York*, starring Gary Cooper.

I came home from the movie and told Dad I was going to join the marines. He advised me to wait and see if the Army Air Corps would lower their requirements for pilot training. We had talked about this before. In fact, that is why I had not gone back to college for the 1941–42 school year. Everybody knew we were headed for war. So I had held on to my summer job at the Johns-Manville factory in St. Louis, making asbestos shingles and siding. The factory worked three shifts to keep up with the military's need for new barracks and warehouses. I worked six days a week, sometimes seven, and the pay was good, more than $50 a week with overtime.

As Dad had predicted, the air corps lowered the entrance requirements for pilot training. A candidate no longer had to be twenty years old with at least two years of college. I was eligible at nineteen, and after passing preliminary physical and written exams at Jefferson Barracks in St. Louis, I could already imagine myself wearing a helmet and goggles. Some forty of us Missourians had qualified. We were placed on fur-

lough while the training center at Kelly Field in San Antonio was cleared
of other trainees to make room for us. The letter we were all waiting for
arrived March 17, 1942.

MEMORANDUM TO: All Cadets on furlough from the
Aviation Cadet Examining Board, 921 New Federal Building,
St. Louis, Mo.
    1. Date of departure from St. Louis, Missouri to Kelly Field,
Texas is Monday, March 23, 1942 by rail transportation.
    2. You will report to this headquarters at 8:15 A.M.,
March 23, prepared to leave.
    3. Travel by privately owned conveyance will not be
authorized.

John A. Allis,
1st Lieut., FA
Recorder

Mom got up early on the morning I was to leave. She always had to rise
early because she was a nurse, and she and her nurse friend Mrs. Rosen-
barger had a long drive to Barnes Hospital in St. Louis. I was still in bed,
pretending to be asleep. I am sure that Mom knew I was faking—and
why—and she mercifully left without forcing the goodbye I had been
dreading for weeks. Sister Nancy said goodbye and went to school. Dad
drove me to Union Station where the other guys were gathering. He told
me to take care of myself and then drove to work.

The train was not scheduled to leave until late afternoon. To kill
time, most of us went to a matinee at a theater near the station. It was a
movie about Canadian bush pilots who got into the Royal Canadian Air
Force when the war started. It was called *Captains of the Clouds*. James
Cagney was in it.

The train trip gave me time to reflect: Did I really want to fly? It had
not been an ambition of mine—actually, it was Dad's idea. I think he
wished he could have been a pilot. He had taken me to a big air show
in Oklahoma City when I was ten. The star stunt pilot was named Art
Killips. He closed the show with a series of loops performed at very low
altitude. The last loop was timed to occur in front of the grandstand, but
the top of the loop was too low and the pilot could not pull out before
the plane drove into the ground. Watching that fatal crash occur a few
hundred yards in front of me could have soured me on aviation, but it
did not, although it certainly made a lasting impression (why else would
I remember the pilot's name?). The thing that impressed me most,

William Mitchell, Sr., the author's father, with his old Winchester 12-gauge double on his shoulder.

though, was that by the time we made the short drive from the airport to home, newsboys were hawking an "extra" that told the story of the crash.

My mind was not made up on aviation, but going to war was a different matter. I was ready. I had been a gun owner and hunter since I was twelve. Dad and I hunted pheasants, ducks, and geese. In those days a duck hunter could use live decoys. Our hunting partner (more a guide) on the Platte River in Nebraska was Fred Diehl, an older man who had been a market hunter in the days before game laws and bag limits. I graduated from a 20-gauge Winchester pump to a 16-gauge Browning automatic and became a fair wing shooter. Unlike most of the other kids riding the train to Texas, I was not leaving the only town I had ever lived in. Before my family moved to Kirkwood, Missouri, we had lived in Memphis, Tennessee (eight years), Oklahoma City (one and a half years), and Hastings, Nebraska (eight years). I had attended five different grammar schools. Dad, an optometrist, had lost a thriving business in Memphis after the stock-market crash. He was hired as a traveling

The author's sister Nancy in 1945 at their home on Geyer Road in Kirkwood, Missouri, where the family moved in 1945.

salesman by American Optical Company and was given the state of Nebraska as his territory. We would see him on weekends occasionally.

My sister Nancy (six and a half years younger than I) was thirteen when I left for the air corps. She was well past the age when she would beg to be allowed to be "the Jane" when my friends and I played Tarzan (we let her be the chimp), but she and her friends were still inconsequential children, as far as I was concerned. When I came home the children were beautiful young women, a transformation that told me how long I had been away.

Mother gave our home a feeling of permanence no matter how temporary it turned out to be. She enjoyed music and gardening, and she liked to explore new ways to express herself artistically. Metalworking was an early hobby, and some of her work in copper, brass, and silver are family treasures today. Mother encouraged my sister and me to explore the way she did, and so when I was a sixth-grader I begged to be allowed to enroll in a mail-order course in taxidermy. Mother did not only consent, she helped me with the skinning and stuffing and all the unpleasant details of that art until I decided I had had enough.

Jean Marsh Mitchell Allison, the author's mother. She was born in Oklahoma Territory and lived to be 100.

Mother was popular with my friends. They liked to come to our house, where she would add her ideas to whatever we were doing. I could tell by how they reacted to her attention that some of my friends would have been happy to swap mothers with me.

On the train I sat with Kenny Weir, a kid from Webster Groves, a town next door to Kirkwood. We had met while we were taking the exams, and we had since seen some movies together. Kenny had a little stutter but only when he was excited or surprised. He was good company and I liked him. Our mothers had even gotten acquainted and planned to keep in touch.

Riding down to Texas, Kenny and I decided we would stick together until the war was over.

PRE-FLIGHT CENTER

Kelly Field, March and April, 1942

Kelly Field had been an Army Air Corps training field since 1917. It was part of the large concentration of airfields centered around San Antonio. As Thomas Greer writes in volume 1 of *The Army Air Forces in World War II*, the complex "came to include every possible combination of facilities from the luxurious permanence of Randolph Field to the heat-baked tar paper hutments of the Aviation Cadet Center; from the huge shops and concrete ramps of Duncan Field to the cow-pasture sod of auxiliary landing strips. On Kelly Field alone, living quarters included modernistic duplexes, permanent barracks, shacks built during World War I, and a tent city."

Our first meal at Kelly came at midnight about two hours after we got off the train. We entered the mess hall in one long line. To speed things up, they opened a door at the other end of the building and cut the line in two between Kenny Weir and me. I wound up first in the line going in one door, and Kenny was last in the line going in the other door. I did not see him again for more than a year. So much for sticking together until the war was over.

My first message home was a postcard, mailed the day after we arrived.

I found some Kelly Field stationery imprinted with silver wings and used it to write my first real letter.

Dear Folks,
    This is the first opportunity I've had to write you, and I
don't know if I'll be able to find a place to mail it, but I'll try.

a/c W. P. Mitchell
A. C. A. D. ; Company M.
Kelly Field, San Antonio, Tex.

THIS SIDE OF CARD IS FOR ADDRESS

Mrs. W. P. Mitchell
124 Idlewild Place
Kirkwood, Missouri

Dear Folks :   Got down here at 10:00 P. M. last
night (Wednesday night). This place is plenty
big and our bunch is now living in tents
waiting to take exams. We haven't
gotten near the aviation cadet barracks
yet, and won't until we pass the exams,
which will come any day. We'll all
receive fatigue uniforms and crew
haircuts today. Lots of food around, and
it's not bad at all. I will send address as soon
as I get one   Love Billy

Postcard announcing the author's arrival at Kelly Field, Texas.

All of the fellows in this part of the field are just newly inducted
men, and this whole section is just an induction center. The
aviation cadet barracks are a little ways away, and we have to
pass our exams, which are coming up in a few days, before we
can go there. The advanced flying field is right adjacent to my
tent and there are planes in the air all day and most of the
night. There is more food around here than we have time to
eat and it's all good. Well, so long until the next letter. Write me

a/c W. P. Mitchell, A.C.R.D. Company M, Kelly Field, San
Antonio, Texas.

> Love to all,
> Billy

Three days later, exams were over (presumably), and I had been moved
from "tent city" to the cadet barracks. Total euphoria.

Dear Folks,

I'm so happy and pleased with this man's army that I'm dele-
rious. Maybe you can tell it in the letter. Everything is swell:
food, uniforms, buddies, climate, barracks, and everything else.
We left tent city today and moved up here to the pre-primary
ground school. Here we have tough upperclassmen and really
eat dirt, but it's worth it. We'll be here five weeks, unless we
wash out. Food is perfect, but we have lots of restrictions while
we're eating it. We must sit only on the first four inches of the
chair, sit straight, and not put our hands on the table. If we
want someone to pass the beans, we say, "Sir, will you pass the
beans, please?" We cannot talk unless we are asking for food.
We have certain ways to lay our silverware when we are
through, and the whole eating procedure is complicated and
keeps us thinking. I've been brushing up on my algebra whenever I get a chance, but here's what I think will take place. I will
not wash out during these first five weeks, because they want to
keep us around until primary, where we get our first flying.
Maybe we are dumb, and ignorant, but if we can fly, they will
make flying sergeants out of us. I'll be around for quite a
while—I hope. I never did memorize my serial number, and at
first I had a little trouble, but this morning I got it and memo-
rized it and feel better. Don't do any worrying about me. All
I'm doing is eating, sleeping, learning, building muscle, and
having a good time. I'm so happy, I can't sit still hardly, so I'm
off again—

Goodbye, and write soon!

> Love to all,
> Billy

It took less than two weeks for cadet officers to instill in me a clannish
pride in my unit. I also developed a pride in myself that could be insuf-

ferable. (I claim in the letter that my rifle weighs ten pounds. Actually it weighed eight-and-a-half pounds.)

> I just finished afternoon drill—three hours of it, with ten-pound rifles. We have learned the manual of arms, and I am recognized as an outstanding exponent of the snappy way to perform the manual, to put it modestly. Yesterday I had to get out in front of a bunch of fellow flight members and show them the technique. It's making me pretty cocky. Saturday, which is army day, we are all going into San Antonio to give a big parade, so we are getting a lot of intensive drill, and I sure do like it. I am really lucky, as I said before, to be in this particular "flight." We've got more esprit de corps than all the other flights, and we are really proud of our prowess on the drill field, and our all-round good appearance. There are fifty-five men in Flight C, and about ten of them are ex-servicemen—former sergeants, lieu-tenants, and corporals. They know how to give commands, make us respect them, and, above all, they have made us take an interest in our work. It really makes me feel good to know that I'm one of the fifty-five best men out of the three thousand on the hill. Of course, all of the drill in the world isn't going to help me fly a plane, but it's fun and a good thing to know.

Hazing was part of the cadet experience for the first six months. Hazing rituals were traditions. They had been kept alive for years, passed down from West Point to Randolph and then from one class to another. Some hazing was quite sophisticated.

> Night before last, the upperclassmen visited our barracks for the first time, and, boy, was it an evening! About four of them walked in all of a sudden when we were sitting around in our pajamas and underwear. We all came to attention immediately, and then they started in on us. First, we had air raids. When the upperclassmen yelled air raid, we had to be under our bunks in three seconds, and if it was a serious air raid, we had to jump between the springs and the mattress. If we didn't make it in three seconds, we were dead, and had to have a funeral. Four guys would pick up the dead man, lay him on a table, and then all the rest of the fellows would walk around the table weeping in their shirttails. I have never laughed so hard in my life when all these big ex-football players and "big ten" wrestling champs

had to fly around the room with arms outstretched and lips sputtering like an airplane. I finally laughed too hard, and they made me get up on a table and drop bombs. It was terrible. Last night they came again, and I was a cat and had to get down on all fours, and chase another guy who was a mouse, all around the beds and tables. That was because I couldn't keep from laughing again.

Appearing in public in uniform for the first time was a thrill. I was fascinated by San Antonio.

Dear Folks,

Yesterday we had our first day off, and the whole bunch of cadets converged on San Antonio. I never saw so many uniforms in my life. There were all of us cadets, about six thousand, and there were thousands of army men from Fort Sam Houston, also sailors and coast guardsmen from Houston and Corpus Christi. We cadets had the edge in uniforms, so we got most of the attention.

San Antonio's main hotel, the Gunter, has reserved its mezzanine floor exclusively for cadets, and that's where we congregate. It's called the "Cadet Club," and we pay for the rent, music, entertainment, etc., out of our monthly check. I think it costs about $1.50 per cadet.

I went through the Alamo again, went out to an amusement park, and just generally circulated around. It's really fun to walk down a crowded street, saluting colonels and taking in all the admiring glances of the women.

I really thought I was the hot stuff.

Saturday was the day of our big parade, and my morale hit a new high when we marched down San Antonio's main drag with the people cheering, and the sergeants barking commands, and the band playing "Semper Fidelis." The reviewing stand was right up against the Alamo, and we all did an "eyes right," and you should've heard the cheers. Boy, I tingled all over.

I consider myself to be pretty lucky to be in the squadron and flight that I am in. This evening we had a big review out here at the post, and the Ninth Squadron was adjudged the crack drill squadron. It is a well-known fact, and has even been admitted by our squadron commander, that Flight C is the outstanding flight in the Ninth Squadron. Element (file) Four in

Flight C is the best element in the flight, and I'm an outstanding rifle wrestler in Element Four, so when you boil it all down, I'm almost a celebrity. Seriously, though, we do have a swell flight, and most of the credit goes to our cadet lieutenant. He was a captain at New Mexico Military Academy, which is one of the best. And before he came here, he was a second lieutenant at Fort Bliss, and he's only nineteen.

Well, I'm pretty fagged, so I guess I'll shower and go to bed. I shave every night too, and some guy asked me why I did.

Well, write soon,

Love,
Billy

I felt out of touch with news of the war. How could I have missed General Doolittle's Raid on Tokyo? It happened on April 19, two weeks before I wrote this letter. In the Philippines, the fighting in Bataan Province was over. The Americans and Filipinos who had retreated to Corregidor Island had surrendered to the Japanese. The infamous "Death March" to the prison camp had just been completed. That stirred us up.

Dear Folks,

This one will be short, because I just got a bunch of shots in the arm and it's killing me.

We all got the shots this noon, and this afternoon we had regular parade, and you should've seen the cadets keel over. We stood at rigid attention for thirty minutes in the hot sun, and guys were dropping all around me. I had to move up four places in my file to fill in places vacated by guys who had passed out. I saw spots myself, but I wiggled my toes like everything, and that kept the blood circulating, so I kept on my feet.

I'm doing OK in school, even in math, so I'm getting more confident. The first math exam that we had netted me a sixty percent, which wasn't so hot, but I got ninety percent in an algebra exam today.

I can identify forty-five American, British, German, and Jap planes now by silhouettes, and we get an exam in that tomorrow.

We get less information on the war than anybody, and sometimes it's hard to imagine that a war is going on. But when we heard about Bataan, it sobered everybody, and a lot of the fellows, especially the ones who had friends in the Philippines, voiced the hate that everybody feels for the Japs, and we all shook on it. It made me tingle as usual, and I'm glad that this squadron, and this flight, is going to be right together from here on out. It's really a swell bunch of guys, and I pity the Japs when McGinnis, Murphy, McLain, McConnell, McCarthy, McIvern, McDonald, Mullins, O'Shaunnessy, and Mitchell take after them.

Write soon, and I still get hungry around 9 P.M.

Love to all,
Billy

What follows is the last letter from pre-flight. With that phase of training behind us, we would move on to primary (primary flight training), where instructors would find out if we could fly. This letter was written in two stages: the first, the night before three major exams; the second, the night following, with exams successfully completed.

Dear Folks,

Tomorrow I have three big exams coming up in navigation, army organization, and battleship identification. They're all very tough, and if I flunk any one of them, I have to stay here for another five weeks. We are scheduled to leave for primary on the twenty-seventh, and I might go to Sikeston, or Parks Field, or Dallas, or about five other places.

[The following night] Dear Folks,

I passed all of my exams, and got a hundred in Naval Identification and Navigation—boy, do I feel good!

Here's some more big news. I will go to Uvalde, Texas, (sixty miles southwest of here) for primary, and will leave here probably Monday. My whole flight will be together down there.

I thought this place was very nice, but a captain told us today that the field at Uvalde is like a country club compared to the replacement center. We will probably fly Stearmans, which are supposed to fly themselves practically. On the dismal side of the picture, there is the fact that 50 percent of the cadets entering primary flunk out. If a man can get through primary, he is all set, because the percentage of washouts in basic and advanced is something like 3 or 4 percent.

I sure do feel nice and relaxed tonight with all those exams finished, and no shots since Wednesday. I have been studying as hard as I ever did in college, and I know all classes of Jap and U.S. naval vessels, and can identify them by little things like the number of turrets, or the deck line, or the type of mast, etc. It's just a lot of hard memorizing, and it keeps a guy busy. This cadet lieutenant of my flight, whom I have mentioned before, well, his dad was once the commander of the aircraft carrier *Saratoga.*

There are some real characters in Flight C, like Murphy, for instance. He studied for seven years to be a priest, and then joined the air corps. He has a real pretty voice, and when he sings in the shower, it sounds swell. There's some song about "How Ireland Got Its Name" that is beautiful, and Murph really puts his heart into it.

Also, there is another character called Mullins. He is a little short guy from Arkansas. He worked in oil fields for years and he's hard as nails, and tough as they come, but he is a member of the Book-of-the-Month Club, and he reads each book like a demon. The last one was *Cross Creek* by Marjorie Rawlings, and he says it is swell.

Well, I'm going to really relax tonight by taking in a show at the post theater with Murphy. It's *Captains of the Clouds,* and I've already seen it, but it's worth seeing again.

Here's some more dope, straight from the captain. After we get our commissions, we will not get any combat flying for at least a year. There won't be a Jap plane in the air by that time. I actually regret it.

Love to all,
Billy

PRIMARY FLIGHT SCHOOL

Garner Field, April to July, 1942

Garner Field at Uvalde was one of the more than fifty "contract" schools authorized to train aviation cadets. The field was named after John Nance Garner, the colorful Uvaldean who was vice president under Franklin D. Roosevelt and who proclaimed the office he held as "not worth a bucket of warm spit."

Three months after Pearl Harbor, the city passed a bond election to purchase 575 acres of mesquite and cactus for an airfield. Four months later, federal approval was granted to build the base. Hangar Six, a fixed-base aviation operator in San Antonio, took over management of the school. There were 125 flight instructors (at the peak of activity) and a support staff of 250. The first class of cadets arrived in January, 1942. My class, 42-J, was the second to train there. It was like moving into a brand-new house.

Here our number one job was to learn how to fly, though we continued to be students of things we were expected to know as air corps officers. What really mattered was how we performed in the cockpit. Our primary flight training at Uvalde encompassed sixty flight hours. At least half of those hours were solo, and each of us made at least 175 landings before we left.

Flying training here was divided into four segments: the *pre-solo* phase, with emphasis on learning the airplane, forced landings, and stall and spin recovery; an *intermediate* phase, focusing on flying standard courses or patterns, such as "8s" and chandelles; an *accuracy* phase, emphasizing proficiency in landings and landing approaches; and an *acrobatic* phase, introducing maneuvers such as loops, Immelmann turns, snap rolls, and slow rolls.

We soon found out if we had what it took to be a pilot. The qualities required had been spelled out in 1936 in a book titled *The Flying Game*. Its author H. H. "Hap" Arnold, who soon became commanding general of the Army Air Forces, was convinced that there is a "flying type." He describes a person so endowed as being "of good moral fiber . . . honest, truthful, reliable" and possessed of "the *sine qua non*, courage." Arnold states, "Few boys who are effeminate or unmanly get called. Those who are sullen, morose or antagonistic in personality are generally rejected. The frank, open-faced, pleasant-mannered, serious-minded, cooperatively-inclined boy is the one who is wanted and the one who is selected nine times out of ten. Any boy who knows in his heart that he is entirely out of step with the ideal flying candidate as pictured here is simply wasting his time in applying for training with Uncle Sam."

I doubt if any of us had read General Arnold's book. It was just as well. We were already eaten up with uncertainty. As Eugene Fletcher describes in his book *"Mister." The Training of an Aviation Cadet in World War II.* "Uncertainty. That was what cadet training was all about."

After Kelly, this base really did look like a country club. The supreme luxury: air-conditioned quarters! Evaporative coolers work beautifully in hot and dry southwest Texas.

> Dear Folks,
>
> I'm sorry that I couldn't complete that phone call. I tried three times, but I didn't have any luck. You see, we have lots of formations that we must make, and I would have to telephone between formations, and every time I called, they told me that it would take from three to four hours to complete the call, and I was supposed to be in bed by that time. I'd be safe in saying that it was impossible to make a long distance call to St. Louis when I tried.
>
> This Uvalde is really the nutz! There are eight men to a suite, and the suite consists of a study room with individual desks, chairs, and lamps, wall lockers, and shelves; a bedroom with eight big beds (maple); a bathroom with four sinks, and swell showers. The outside of our barracks looks exactly like "Cal-Aero" did in *Keep 'Em Flying*. It is landscaped, with showers [a sprinkler system] all over the lawns, and porches running the

The author in his aviation cadet uniform at the preflight school, Kelly Field, Texas, March, 1942.

length of the barracks. We have a blue-tiled swimming pool, and a beautiful PX and recreation room.

We were issued blue gabardine coveralls, silk-lined, zipper front, and big patch pockets. We also got helmets and goggles and mechanics cap and coveralls.

I will go up for the first time with my instructor tomorrow, probably. He will zoom around and after a while let me take the controls for a few minutes, even though I don't know a thing about it. That ought to be exciting.

Our planes are Fairchild PT-19s and they really look racey. Low-wing monoplanes with 175 horsepower and a top speed of 120 mph. They look a lot like a real pursuit plane, a P-40.

I thought that they were tough on us at Kelly, but this place is twice as bad. Everything has to be perfect, and if it isn't, we walk the ramp, as they call it. It means that we walk at attention for hours while everybody else is in town enjoying themselves.

About all I've done today is sit around shining shoes and brass buttons and insignias.

My roommates are a former first lieutenant, a former second lieutenant (he was our flight lieutenant at Kelly—the one whom I raved about so much), a former gunner in a patrol bomber (sank a sub at Aruba), and four other guys about my speed. They were all in my flight at Kelly, and we're well acquainted. Murphy is in the next suite and we get together as much as possible.

We have a public-address system that has loudspeakers in all the suites and all over the field. The usual command is "Cadet so-and-so, report at your own convenience—in one minute!"

All we new arrivals are known as "dodos," and we'll be dodos until we solo.

There are quite a few South American students here from Argentina and Brazil. They bend over backward trying to be good neighbors, and the instructors try to be good neighbors by not washing them out unless they are utterly hopeless. There are only about two hundred students here altogether, and that makes it pretty nice.

I just got a package from Aunt Jonnie. They announced it over the PA system, "Attention, Mr. W. P. Mitchell—a package has just arrived for you. On the double, Mr. Mitchell!" The package was a chocolate cake, and it's sure nice.

We had a personal inspection this evening at retreat, and I did OK. In fact, a bunch of the inspecting officers said, "Very nice brass, Mr. Mitchell." It made me feel pretty good.

We don't get any destructive hazing here from the upper-classmen—it's all constructive.

For instance, when we turn a corner at any time, walking between barracks or to mess, we must first turn our head and look over our shoulder in the direction we're turning. It's called looking into a turn. If we can form that habit, we won't be colliding with any other planes when we are in the air. It's a good habit to form.

Boy, my shower bath schedule has been shot to pieces. I haven't taken a bath since I left Kelly three days ago. I've tried a couple of times, but when I'm all set, the bugle sounds and I have to do my best to make the formation on time.

I have about $80.00 on my hands now, and I would like to send some of it home. Would you refresh my memory as to how to send it? I don't get to a bank, so should I send a money order from the post?

Also, I would like to get a camera, because we can take pictures of anything around here, and there is some swell scenery. If you can get a discount on an Argus Candid Camera, that would be about what I want.

A couple of weeks ago there were some *Collier's* photographers out here taking pictures for an article that will appear soon. We have been told that Uvalde has the highest ranking of any primary field in the United States, and I know for sure that the outstanding civilian instructor is stationed here, so I'm getting the best available.

Love,
Billy

Dear Folks,

I've been up twice now and I have one hour and ten minutes to my credit. It's really swell but it's a lot of work. Yesterday I practiced turns, climbing turns, and gliding turns. They sound easy but it has to be just exactly right or the instructor yells my ears off.

The first time I went up we climbed up to five hundred feet and the instructor said, "Have you got your right hand on the stick, left hand on the throttle, and both feet on the rudder pedals?" I nodded my head, yes. Then he said, "Well, I hope you have, because I haven't!" Boy, I broke out in a cold sweat, but I eased up after a while.

After another few hours, they will begin to wash us out in a hurry. There are about five guys in my squadron that toss their cookies (vomit) every time they go up, and there are a few others that aren't coordinated well enough to ever learn to fly. They will go first, and then they will pick off the guys that aren't showing enough progress. Everybody is worried and nobody can understand how on earth he will ever solo, including me. But some of us are bound to, so I'm going to try to be one of them.

My instructor bawls me out through little tubes (gosports) attached to the ear flaps on my helmet, and I can't talk back

because he couldn't hear me anyway. Our planes are swell
and easy to control and, boy, do I get a terrific appetite up in
the air!

In three minutes, I have call to quarters and must start
studying for an hour and a half, so I'll close this letter and write
again soon.

Love to all,
Billy

As any pilot knows, the relationship between stick and rudder is criti-
cal. This is especially true in a turn. Apply too much rudder and the airplane skids. Too much stick and the airplane slips. Apply the right
amount of each and the turn is smooth. It's a landmark moment when
the student discovers how silky smooth the airplane will respond when
the controls are well coordinated.

Dear Folks,

Today I am walking on clouds. Boy, I really feel good, and
it's all because of a few nice words from my instructor. We went
up this morning and started working on turns and banks, about
the toughest things to get perfect. I've been just doing fair on
turns and banks, but today the exact coordination between
stick and rudder hit me all of a sudden, and my instructor really
gave me a hand. He said, "Well, Mitchell, you've finally caught
on. Now, if everyone else would catch on, I could get some
sleep at night." Boy, I really felt happy.

Also today we practiced our first stalls and, boy, they really
give you a sensation. Here's the way the common, power-on
stall works:

The first time I tried it, I pushed the stick too far forward,
and we went into a vertical dive and flooded the carburetor, but
my instructor just laughed and kept on doing stalls until I came
out of one right. Boy, when I come out of that dive, it feels like
someone is mashing me down through my seat.

Last Friday during study period, from 8:00 till 9:30 P.M.,
our cadet major came in and told us that it was OK if we wrote
letters during that time, just so we hid them when an officer
came in.

Love to all,
Billy

AIR CORPS TRAINING DETACHMENT
GARNER FIELD - UVALDE, TEXAS

you point your plane up at a high angle of attack.

when the rate of climb is too much for the power of the plane, the ship starts quivering all over.

and the plane falls straight down, but before it can go into a spin —

I jam the nose down, and give it full throttle —

and then pull it out of the dive, and ease the throttle back to cruising speed.

Excerpt from a letter from primary flight school in which the author diagrams "how the common, power-on stall works."

Dear Folks,

The queerest, most unusual and the most lucky thing happened to a St. Louis cadet today. I'll describe it in detail.

This guy's name is Sexton, and he's a dodo like me. He was up this afternoon and was making some pretty sloppy turns. His instructor got mad and jerked the stick away from him, and put the plane in a steep bank, then rolled it level and into a dive. Mr. Sexton's safety belt was not fastened, and he sailed right out of the plane into the air. The plane was at five hundred feet when he fell out, and that's two hundred feet below the minimum distance usually required for a successful jump. However, Mr. Sexton's chute opened at two hundred feet, and he landed OK. He went to a farmhouse, called the field, and was back in an hour. As soon as he returned, they took him up for a confidence ride so he wouldn't get leery of an airplane. After they had flown for about fifteen minutes a piston broke and they had to make a forced landing in the very same field that Mr. Sexton had previously landed with his parachute, and they called the field from the same farmhouse. They sent an ambulance after them and as a final ironic touch, the ambulance ran out of gas on the way back.

Now isn't that one for Ripley? After all that he's been through, Mr. Sexton is perfectly well, except for a little scratch on his hand.

I thought at first that I wouldn't tell you about this because you might worry, but there isn't any need to worry because that is the first jump and first forced landing that has been pulled here in months, and besides, I am one guy that doesn't forget his safety belt. Also, I made a practice forced landing today that my instructor said was as pretty as a picture. And, in addition, I have an instructor who doesn't lose his temper and flip the plane around.

I'd better start studying now because there is a terrific navigation test coming up tomorrow and I'm not too sharp in that stuff.

> Love to all,
> Billy

This letter followed a telegram I had sent as soon as I could get to a phone. The telegram had stated simply: "Soloed today." The letter fills in the details.

Dear Folks,

Yesterday I became a man—I soloed, and I think it was the happiest day of my life. In my last letter I told you how poorly I flew on Saturday, and how worried I was. Well, on Monday it was just the opposite—I just couldn't do anything wrong, but my instructor didn't crack a smile. After about three practice landings, we taxied over to the safety zone and he climbed out of the cockpit and said, "Mitchell, I've got a wife and two kids and I'll be darned if I'll go up with you again today. Take it up by yourself!" Those were the sweetest words I've ever heard. I didn't have any trouble with my solo hop, but the plane sure handled easier with his weight out of the nose. After I got down, he congratulated me and said that the landing that I made just before I soloed was really pretty. He said that I'll probably never make a better landing in my life. I guess I was just hot yesterday, and I hope I stay that way.

When we solo we are entitled to wear our goggles up on our helmets, instead of around our necks when we are on the ground, and we wear a little pair of wings on our flight caps.

We really had a storm last night and this morning the field is too soggy for flying. There was a lot of lightning also, and something happened to the lights, so we had breakfast in total darkness.

While I'm on the subject of food, I'd like to tell you about what they feed us here. It is really poor food; in fact, it's about the worst I ever ate. I can't understand why, because everything else is so swell.

A Beechcraft twin-engine trainer had to make a forced landing here last night during the storm. It just took off a few minutes ago. Anytime a strange plane comes in here, everybody runs down to the flight line and looks it over just like a bunch of small town folks look over a strange car.

If you can find a camera like I want, at a discount, I sure would appreciate it, because I can get some swell pictures here.

I'll write again soon.

Love to all,
Billy

The following letter was mailed on May 30. About three weeks had passed since I went up for the first time. My total flying time (dual and solo) as of this letter is probably about twenty hours. Forty more hours here and we move on to basic flying training. Meanwhile, good friends are being eliminated. Murphy's departure really hurts.

Dear Folks,

Today I flew for two and a half hours—thirty-five minutes dual, and the rest was solo. Boy, I really am fagged out tonight. Flying is the most strenuous job that I ever took on. A guy has to be on his toes all the time, and there are so many things to watch. Besides watching instruments, wind direction, other planes, etc., we have to look out for buzzards. Those darned birds are flying around at all altitudes, and they could do some damage if they hit a plane. I had my accuracy landing stages to-day, and the idea is to hit a line when you land, or else bracket the line—that is land on one side within a fifty-foot radius and the next time land on the other side. I hit the line four times, and got a twenty-two, and perfect is twenty-one, so I'm walking on clouds tonight, or rather I would be if I wasn't so tired.

For the last few days I've been going out solo about ten miles from the airport and practicing everything except spins. My instructor won't let me do spins by myself yet, because I still scare him when I try to come out of one. I do stalls though, and that's a thrill.

My solo time is now seven hours and one minute—I really built it up today.

Boy, this flying is more fun. I get up there alone and imagine all kinds of things. For instance, I say that the other planes are Japs and I zoom around and try to get a bead on them. I can see myself in the rearview mirror in the front cockpit, and that helps.

We are all brown as Indians now, and it looks pretty good. That old sun really beats down when we're up in the air with no shade.

Murphy left yesterday, and I just about broke down. Boy, I hated to see that guy go. He is just about perfect, and I hope you all can meet him some day.

Well, study time—so, so long.

Love to all,
Billy

Dear Folks,

I just called you about five minutes ago, and while every-thing is fresh in my mind, I think I'll write a letter.

It sure was nice to hear you all—I guess I was pretty lucky to have called when everyone was at home.

Well, in about a week at the longest, the present upper class will move on to Randolph Field, and we will become upperclassmen. They will move in a new bunch of dodos for us to harass. We will get some sweet revenge.

Yesterday, they picked a group of us dodos, and from that group will come our new cadet officers. We had tryouts for two hours, and during that entire time, we were either standing at attention or marching at attention. They took each one of us individually and gave us a certain maneuver to perform with the squad of men, consisting of about thirty or thirty-five. I got out there, and our commandant of cadets told me to put the First Element where the Third Element was, and the Third Element where the Second Element was, without making the men break ranks or move more than six paces. Boy, I was stymied, and so were all the other guys, because when he asked if anyone could do it, he got no answer. Then I had the guys do some facing movements, and that was all. I'll be lucky if I get any rank at all, but I don't want to be a cadet officer anyway, so it makes no difference.

I told you over the phone about this business of leaving landing flaps down, but I didn't make it very clear, so I'll explain just what happened.

When we come in for a landing, we use landing flaps on our wings to slow our speed down, otherwise we'd be coming in about as fast as a P-40. We lower these flaps as we glide in, and as soon as we stop on the ground, we're supposed to put the flaps back up to their regular position. If we forget this little detail, we are compelled to wear a big red sling on our left arm for twenty-four hours. I forgot two days in a row, and I had to wear the sling for forty-eight hours. I think that cured me though, because it's sure humiliating to wear that sling.

Yesterday I flew a brand-new ship that had not been flown before except on the test flight. It was really keen. It controlled just right, and it really had power.

The more I go up by myself, the more relaxed I become. Saturday I did a lot of singing and gawking around. What's really fun is when some other dodo that I know, who is also soloing, is flying alongside of me. We wave back and forth, or dip our wings—it sure is fun.

The landing pattern can get pretty tricky when the wind tee is not parallel with the field. You see, we must fly parallel with the tee all the time that we are in the pattern. Besides the tee, we must watch our speed, altitude, RPMs, other planes, and make sure that our turns and landings are precise. Come to think of it, I don't see how I ever remember my flaps, with all that other stuff on my mind.

Do you ever remember seeing those frames with a canvas sheet stretched out, and attached to springs? They have them in circuses a lot, and gymnasts get on them and bounce around. They call them trampolines. That's always appealed to me, and we happen to have one here. This morning another guy and I went out, and had a lot of fun on one. You just give a little jump on the canvas and the springs throw you way up in the air.

Our swimming pool opened Friday, but the swimming was so restricted by military discipline that it wasn't any fun. We line up on the edge of the pool at attention when we do calisthenics. After that, we pair off with a buddy, and every five minutes the instructor blows his whistle, and the buddies must hold each other's hand up to show that they're together. I had a buddy that couldn't swim. I wouldn't be a bit surprised if the instructor would say, "Attention! In cadence, swim!!"

I guess this letter is long enough, so I'll sign off. Write soon.

Love to all,

Billy

P.S. I'm enclosing some money to take care of the call.

I have just become an upperclassman, which means I am authorized to harass dodos. I am finally free to get some payback for the hazing I endured as an underclassman. But among the dodos just bused in are six cadets from West Point. They have already spent three years at the U.S. Military Academy, learning how to be generals. Now they are here to learn how to be pilots. They are dodos, all right. But underclassmen? Not exactly.

Dear Folks,

Well, an awful lot has happened in the last two days, and it has all been very enjoyable.

Yesterday we became upperclassmen and they moved in 135 dodos for us to heckle, and today we were paid, and I received

$154.19 in good cold cash. I still have quite a bit left from the last partial payment, so I'll send the bulk of it home right away by money order.

Boy, am I having fun with these dodos—they're mostly Brooklyns and they're really off the beam. It gives me particular pleasure to bawl out a Brooklyn dodo.

My flying is progressing as well as my instructor expects—I think. Today I flew for two hours and thirty-one minutes, and I was so tired this afternoon that I felt like I'd been drugged or something. It seems unusual that two and a half hours of sitting on a nice soft parachute could tire a man out so bad, but, believe me, it sure does.

During the last few days they've been moving in quite a few transferees from the Royal Canadian Air Force, and today we got six new dodos from West Point. The West Pointers have had three years at WP, but they will be just as much dodos as anyone else. I can't quite see myself bawling out a West Pointer, but might have to.

We flew this morning, and there were quite a few thundershowers scattered over the area. It was really fun dodging those big black clouds in my little PT-19A.

In our planes here at Garner Field, we use 88-octane gasoline, and it's the highest grade gasoline used at any primary school in the United States. Most other schools use 65-octane, and the P-39s and P-38s in actual combat use 100-octane, which isn't much better. We really have the "get-up-and-go" in these little planes.

It's time to take a shower now, so I'll try to get through before "Taps"—I haven't made it yet.

Love to all,
Billy

P.S. Here's the money for the phone call. I'll try to remember to enclose it this time.

I have almost thirty hours' flying time. But when it comes to engines, I am still a dodo.

Dear Folks,

Here I am again. The main reason for this letter is to send you the money for the phone call, which I have forgotten just twice already (sometimes I wonder how I can fly a plane), and to ask you to send me my radio whenever you have any spare time. It probably needs some repairing, but there isn't any hurry, because I know how busy you all are.

Here at Garner Field, we are teetotally isolated from all news, music, and everything. We never hear about those bombing raids unless we read it in the paper, and this San Antonio paper is lousy. Boy, a radio would be a lifesaver. We have a lot more fun time since we are upperclassmen, and that makes a radio more practical.

I just flew for an hour and one minute today, and it was all solo. Nothing unusual happened so I won't bother telling you about it. Just about two more hours' flying time and I will have thirty hours—enough for a civilian private license. And my thirty hours mean a lot more than a civilian's thirty hours, because we fly 175-horsepower planes, instead of a 45- or 50-horsepower Cub or Taylorcraft.

Well, I have a test in engines tomorrow and also a test in meteorology, so I'd better do a little studying so I can get "class A privileges," which I don't have now. These engines are still Greek to me, but I'm beginning to see the light. Today we traced the lubricating system through a PT-19A, and, boy, was it complicated. Good night.

Love to all,
Billy

The following letter introduces my "bay buddies," the six cadets with whom I share a suite. The backgrounds I attribute to one or two look too good to be true. But they were intelligent and mature young men. As the youngest and the least sophisticated, I was known as "the kid." It did not bother me a bit. I respected these guys. Dick Misner looked me up a few weeks after the war ended. We had lunch at the Park Forest Hotel in St. Louis, and my little sister Nancy came along. I believe Dick made an effort to locate and get in touch with all of his Uvalde bay buddies at that time. I do not know how successful he was.

Dear Folks,

I passed my second school check today, and, believe me, I really feel happy, and I think my instructor does too. I was up for forty-four minutes, and we went through stalls, spins, lazy eights, chandelles, forced landing, pylon eights.

I've really improved on my forced landings, because today on my check ride I had one, and when I was still at a thousand feet after gliding down from twenty-five hundred, my check pilot said, "Take me home, Mitchell—your pattern is perfect—you couldn't miss!"

Please excuse my cockiness, I just feel pretty gay tonight.

Yesterday the heat got up to 111 degrees, and today it was just as bad. This heat makes the engines conk out for some reason. They run OK up in the air, but on the ground when we are taxiing, we have to keep working on the emergency pressure pump or the engine will quit. Mine quit today way on the other side of the field, and I had to get a mechanic over there to give me a crank. Boy, I felt silly.

Flying is becoming automatic to us all now. We don't have to look at instruments much anymore, and when we do, we can cover the whole instrument board in a quick glance. We just listen and can tell if we're cruising right, and rudder pedals and stick coordination is really getting smooth. I really think I can handle a plane better than I could ever drive a car.

Mom, your picture is really nice, and I'm sure glad to get it. I took a roll of swell pictures of me all decked out in flying togs sitting all over an airplane, and I was really expecting some nice pictures. I got them back the other day, and all there was, was eight black squares where the pictures should've been. Something must be wrong with the camera, and I'm going to have it looked over. Your pictures came out OK.

I think I'll introduce you to my bay mates. Our bay is the best bay at Garner Field any way you look at it. Our percentage of washouts is by far the lowest—only one out of eight. We are well represented by cadet officers—more officers of higher rank than any other bay. Here are my bay buddies.

George Merz, 21 years old; two years as gunner and engineer on big bomber in Trinidad and Panama; sank Nazi sub at Aruba; home is Jersey City, N.J.

Paul Meyer, 26 years old, was first lieutenant in coast artillery; lived in Hastings for two years. Home is Washington, D.C.

John Miller, 20 years old; ex-second lieutenant in cavalry at Fort Bliss. Father was commander of aircraft carrier, *Saratoga.* Home: Kansas City.

Gail Miller, 23 years old, from Toledo, Ohio; darned good guy.

Dick Misner, 21 years old, a rookie like me; classy swimmer; good guy. Home: Des Moines, Iowa.

Fred Moody, 25 years old, another rookie. Home: Taft, Texas. He looks like the typical Texan.

Well, now you know who I live with. They're a classy bunch of guys, and we sure have fun together. Maybe you can meet them sometime.

It's time to go to bed now, so I'll close for tonight. I feel more confident tonight about surviving primary than at any time. Basic and advanced are question marks, but I think I have primary whipped.

If we could sleep longer, and if our food was better, this would be a paradise. It's not bad in its present state.

Well, I'll head for the shower now and do my best to beat "Taps" tonight.

Love to all,
Billy

This letter describes our first cross-country flight. I also tell the folks that I have enough confidence in my flying to have invested in a pilot's logbook. Most cadets (maybe all of them) had logbooks by this time. A civilian employee entered our flight time in our books when we logged it.

Dear Folks,

Well, I'm sitting here listening to my little radio and feeling pretty fine. Everything seems to be going as smooth as I could wish, and we had a good supper tonight. Who could ask for more?

I had my cross-country today and it wasn't so smooth—it was pretty rough. It was a 150-mile trip both ways, and our instructors rode with us to make sure that we all got back. We flew down to Asherton, Texas, followed the Rio Grande over to Eagle Pass, and then back to Garner Field. We used a compass and checkpoints in following our course. One of my checkpoints was a large water hole way out in the mesquite between Asherton and Eagle Pass. When I got down there, I saw water holes as far as I could see all across the landscape. I couldn't figure out just which water hole I wanted, so I just had to stick to my compass. It was a lot of fun, though, flying over strange country in a loose formation with several other planes.

Tomorrow I will get acrobatics, and I'm sure looking forward to it. Loops and snap rolls are supposed to be easier than falling off a log, but slow rolls are pretty tough.

Yesterday we all were issued brand-new officer's type gas masks, and we had gas mask drill also. We march along, and when the lieutenant says, "Gas!" we all stop and fly into our masks. It was a lot of fun seeing how fast we could get into the masks. The fastest we could do it in our first drill was fifty seconds, but that isn't bad for beginners.

Bud sure must've drawn a lemon when he went to Sumter for basic flight school. I was mistaken when I told you that all of the guys from Garner went to Randolph. Our upper class went to San Angelo, Randolph, Waco; Lake Charles, Louisiana; and Enid, Oklahoma. However, we will probably go to Randolph. I don't think I'll like Randolph. They have organized hazing there, and it's terrible. I got all I could stand here, and it's much worse at Randolph. All the basic schools down here are really nice and modern—there isn't a chance to draw a lemon.

I have enough confidence in myself now to buy a pilot logbook. I'll give the book to a lady down in the operations building and she will put all of my flying time in it and will keep it up-to-date. It's a nice thing to have around in civilian life as a convincer.

Well, I'd better study now, so I'll close.

I'm going to try to enclose a picture of Garner Field.

Write soon and, Daddy, I can't get off the post to get you a card, but I'll manage something.

I'll send money order as soon as possible.

Love to all,

Billy

P.S. I'm sending our upper class's annual—so you'll get it about the same time as the letter. I'll have to send the picture in a separate package.

I passed the forty-hour mark the day I wrote this letter. Elimination rides continued to take a toll. I reported that my instructor recommended two cadets for elimination the day of this letter. That just left two of us, Art Lynch and me.

Dear Folks,

Well, today I passed forty hours. I have about forty-two hours now. And will have about forty-five or forty-six before the week is over. I flew for two hours and forty minutes today and spent most of my time working on chandelles, lazy eights, and stalls. I'm getting pretty smooth on these maneuvers now, and in a few more hours I'll get slow rolls, snap rolls, loops, vertical reversements, and Immelmanns. Those are the real stunts, but they won't be too hard, because they don't have to be smooth like chandelles or lazy eights. When we do stunts, we can be as rough as we want to—the rougher the better.

It's hard to realize, but I'm getting pretty close to basic. We only get sixty hours in primary. So I have less than twenty to go.

My instructor put two more guys up for elimination today, which makes a total of four men he has disposed of. That just leaves two of us—Art Lynch and me. Lynch and I have been palling around a lot lately, and we're real buddies. He's from Tarrytown, New York, which is just a few miles from where Bud lived.

Boy, it's been hot lately—especially today. A lot of these guys have had previous service in the tropics, down in Panama, Trinidad, and other South American outposts. They say that it's hot down there, but it isn't anything compared to this Uvalde heat. It's really a furnace down here.

I'll try to write again tomorrow night. Thanks a million for the radio and cookies—they both went over with a bang. The radio works fine, and it sure is nice to be abreast of everything again.

Love to all,
Billy

This letter divulges what I know about my instructor. It also reveals the formality that characterized the instructor-cadet relationship. I later discovered that Mr. Sasser was Parnell ("Boots") Sasser and that he had been a crop-duster in Mississippi. He was the "darned good instructor" I claimed him to be. I was lucky to get him. I wasn't so lucky with the "swell girl" I met in town that day. "I imagine you'll be hearing more about her," I wrote. Her name never came up again.

Dear Folks,

Another week has rolled around in a big hurry—the time sure flies down here. I had my first army progress check last week and I made out OK. I went up with Lieutenant Schaefer for just twenty-eight minutes and we went through some maneuvers and came right back down. Yesterday I flew from the front cockpit for the first time, and it was just like learning to fly all over again. Your perception is entirely different in front, especially on landings. I went up with my instructor for fifty-one minutes, and then went up alone and made nine landings, and after that I didn't have any trouble in the front seat—in fact, I can fly better up there than in back. Somebody asked about my instructor—what kind of a guy he was, and where he hails from. He's from Corinth, Mississippi, and he worked in Memphis quite a while. His dad used to be a streetcar conductor there. He's just about my height and has a little blonde mustache, which makes him look funny. I imagine he's around twenty-five or twenty-six years old. He's married and has a family, and they all live in Uvalde. His last name is Sasser—I don't know his first name, because I only address him as "Sir," or "Mr. Sasser." He's crazy about fishing, and he spends his weekends on the local lakes and streams. I like him a lot, and he's a darned good instructor. I went into town this afternoon and I just got back, so I'll continue the letter. While I was in town, I bought a *Collier's,* and was I surprised when I saw an article about cadets illustrated with photographs of Garner Field. The issue of *Collier's* is the one with a man in an oxygen helmet flying a plane on the cover, and the three pictures on the left-hand side of the article were taken at Garner. Foreign student Rodriguez was a pal of mine—we called him Pancho. He's in basic now. The article merits careful reading too. The guy that wrote it knew his onions.

Boy, I sure met a swell girl in town today. She is really nice. Her name is Hazel Clark, and I imagine you'll be hearing more about her. Nancy, I sent you a little present this afternoon, and I hope you'll like it. I won't tell you what it is, but they're pretty popular around here, and I thought this was an unusually nice one. This week I really got off the beam, and collected eleven demerits (gigs). That means I must walk the ramp for six hours next weekend.

Well, I'll be writing again soon. Daddy, I'm glad to see that your new job is coming along in good shape, and I hope you can manage to see the man in San Antonio. I'll be expecting you all down around November, so start planning on it.

Love to all,
Billy

Dear Folks,

Well, primary is all over except for the celebrating and one engines final. I had my last ride in a PT-19A this afternoon, and I made the worst landing I've ever made. I counted six bounces and there were probably more. I felt like a dodo. I think I have accomplished something even if I don't go any further. I feel pretty much at home in a 175-horsepower plane, and I think that I can fly well enough to take care of myself. It makes me feel pretty good to look out my window at the planes sitting on the line and know that I can take one up in the air and bring it down, and even do a few loops or rolls. We've had very rough weather this last week—strong winds and dust that practically blankets the field. We come down and our faces are black except for the circles that our goggles covered. It's a lot of fun and it's the best training possible, because we're going to have it all over the fair-weather pilots. I almost forgot to tell you—we're going to Randolph for basic. Isn't that something? The best pilot training school in the world—the closest thing to West Point that I can think of, and I'm going to be there in a few more days. It's hard to imagine, but it's true. Last Thursday night we had our graduation banquet with all the instructors as guests. Mr. Sasser accumulated two more students who had to change instructors about two weeks ago. Mr. Lynch, these other two fellows, and I bought Mr. Sasser a present, as is the custom around here. It was a nice Seth Thomas clock with a bronze airplane on top, and a plate in front, below the face, with our names engraved on it. Sasser really loved it, so did his wife. They're on their way to Mississippi now for their vacation, and they're taking the clock with them to show the home folks. Last night they had us out to their house for dinner and it was swell. I'd just about forgotten how it was to sit in an easy chair and eat in a real dining room. Mr. Sasser (Parnell "Boots" Sasser) is a perfect guy, and I just wish that I could have him for an instructor through the rest of my training. At Randolph I'll get assigned to some brand-new lieutenant with shiny bars on his shoulders, who thinks that he's due all the respect in the world. We have a couple of them here for check pilots, and they're really a pain in the neck. They cool off after they've been an officer for a while. But right after they've gotten those bars, they're hard to get along with. I guess you know, don't you, Daddy? We're leaving for Randolph on the 4th of July, so I'll be around here for a while yet, but no furlough.

The dance starts in fifteen minutes and I have a date, and haven't even started getting ready yet, so I'd better get ready. Write soon.

> Love to all,
> Billy

BASIC FLIGHT SCHOOL

Randolph Field, July to September, 1942

R andolph Field was dedicated in 1931. It was the first facility in the nation designed to be a permanent air station. The base was laid out in the shape of a wheel instead of the conventional grid. Streets radiated from a central hub. Telephone wires were underground. The entire base was landscaped with indigenous trees and plants. Housing and social facilities were commodious and exemplified style and permanence. Hangars and landing fields were ranged outside the wheel. The entire facility encompassed twenty-three hundred acres. If you were looking for a symbol of the military's belief in the future of aviation, you would find it at Randolph Field.

To my eye, Randolph was an Ivy League college, a West Point on the Hudson, and a Spanish Alcazar all rolled into one. It was dignified and romantic at the same time. Randolph put its imprint on a cadet in many ways. A rather mundane rule, for example, had an exemplary effect. It had to do with the khakis we wore. Before we arrived at Randolph, our khaki shirts and trousers looked essentially like those of any other army noncom. They were relatively new, reasonably well fitting, and usually clean, starched, and pressed. But that was not good enough for Randolph. We were ordered to the cadet tailor shop, first thing. Shirts were snugged in at the waist, trousers at the butt. And for the rest of our stay at Randolph, our khakis were dry-cleaned, not laundered. Dry-cleaning preserved the original nut-brown color of khaki, whereas repeated launderings would have whitened it. Thus the color and cut of his khakis distinguished the Randolph cadet from other cadets—and from anyone else wearing khaki.

The mission at Randolph, as at all basic flying schools, was to make military pilots out of students who had graduated from primary. The student would be expected to operate a heavier, more powerful, and more complex airplane than he had flown in primary. Techniques of instrument flying, night flying, and formation flying would be introduced. This phase of training would require seventy to seventy-five hours of flight time. I arrived at Randolph forewarned that it would be tough. ("You'll hate every minute of it, but you'll always be glad you were here.") I was ready to take anything the school could dish out. I wanted to join the Randolph fraternity almost as much as I wanted wings. My first letter from Randolph, however, indicates that I had some second thoughts.

Dear Folks,

I remember that they put us into a brace as soon as we got off the bus, and I just resumed my normal posture a few minutes ago.

The food is good at Randolph Field, but we don't get any, because we can't even turn our plates over until the upper class is through eating, and by that time it's time to leave. They told me as soon as we arrived that we would hate this place every day we're here, but when we leave, we'll be proud of the fact that we survived Randolph. I can see very clearly just what they mean.

You should see my class tonight. Everybody is in a daze and wondering why places like Randolph are allowed to exist.

The upper class will cool off after this first week, and it should be a lot easier, but this next week, and tomorrow especially, will be a nightmare.

Well, when we get out of here, we should be officer material, so I'll just keep that in mind when I'm all twisted up in a brace (posture correction is what they call it here).

I sent you a couple of pictures and an annual this morning. The pictures aren't so hot, but I think the "Slipstream" [the 42-J classbook from Garner Field] is nice.

Write soon.

Love to all,
Billy

The North American Aviation BT-9 had been around since the mid-1930s. It replaced the Seversky BT-8, which was reputed to be too diffi-

The BT-9 basic trainer felt underpowered and unresponsive to the author.
Illustration courtesy The Cadet Club

cult for cadets at the intermediate stage of flight training. Historian Rebecca Cameron notes, too, that the BT-9 "contributed to the high fatality rate in air training, but it remained in use nonetheless for several more years." The BT-9 was the oldest, klunkiest trainer on the field. It had largely been replaced by the newer and easier-to-fly BT-13s and BT-14s. My contingent of cadets (Hangar G) was the last group at Randolph (maybe anywhere) assigned to BT-9s. Everybody else got BT-13s and BT-14s.

To me, the BT-9 felt heavy, unresponsive, and underpowered, even though it had a 400-horsepower Wright Whirlwind engine. I don't recall the spoken opinions of my fellow cadets regarding the BT-9. But I remember a picture that probably summed up our feelings. It was a cartoon that appeared in our 42-J classbook. It shows an apprehensive cadet peering around the engine of a BT-9. He is looking at a large black buzzard that is sitting on one wing.

Dear Folks,

Five days at Randolph, and I'm just about done in. I am room orderly this week, and all the responsibility for keeping this room clean and inspectable rests on my tired shoulders. Ironically, just as I was writing the above, about my being room orderly, two cadet officers walked in and inspected the room.

They ran their hands over everything looking for dust, etc., but I don't think they found any. But we got gigged anyway, because another officer instructed us to sing "Happy Birthday" when the inspecting officer came in, and the inspecting officer didn't like it and gave us demerits (gigs).

This afternoon I got my first ride in a BT, and it was sure nice. That's the only cheery thing about this place. We fly BT-9s, the oldest and the trickiest ships in the field. At Randolph, there are three types of basic trainers used—BT-14s, BT-13s, and BT-9s. The 14s and the 13s are new ships and are simple to fly, but my instructor said that if you can fly a BT-9, you can fly anything, so here's hoping I can fly one.

Boy, you should see the instrument panel—lights, radio, mixture control, propeller pitch, turn and bank indicator, and all the other standard instruments like we had on our PTs. It's really a maze.

We'll get formation flying, day and night; cross-country, day and night; just plain night flying; and all the standard maneuvers such as we had at primary.

It will be a rough course, but if we can finish it, we'll sure be all set for advanced, because Randolph has a darned good reputation around here.

Well, my books are being neglected, and I have a million other things to take care of, so I'll sign off for tonight. The food here is wonderful and I think I'm gaining back some weight.

Write soon.

Love to all,
Billy

I was off to a bad start at Randolph. The BT-9 airplane was intimidating me. So was my instructor. The following letter is July 12. The Texas heat might have been a downer too. Our barracks were not air-conditioned, as they were in Uvalde. But I cannot blame the heat for my instructor's disposition. He would start each lesson a happy man, singing loudly enough that I could hear without earphones. "I've got spurs that jingle, jangle, jingle." Then he'd segue smoothly into "Goddammit, Mitchell, what do you think you're doing?" This became his mantra.

Dear Folks,

What do you think of this stationery. Pretty nice, isn't it? I got a whole stack of it for one buck.

After today, though, I'm beginning to wonder why I bought so much Randolph Field stationary. If I don't improve my flying in a hurry, I won't be around here much longer. Every day my instructor practically blows up at me, even for the slightest little mistakes, and then I get rattled and make big mistakes.

I know what my trouble is: It takes me a long time to catch on to something, and make it stay in my mind, and that doesn't go around here.

We're supposed to catch on fast, and not need to be told more than one time about anything. Some instructors take extra pains to be patient with their students, and overlook the little mistakes. I didn't get one like that though. He is very impatient and nervous, and when I make a mistake, he practically burns my ears off through the headphones. I'm afraid to use any initiative, because if I don't do a maneuver the way he would do it, I get blasted again. If I can hang on for the next few days and solo, everything will be OK, because it just takes time for me to straighten things out, and I can do that when I'm up alone without him in the backseat. If I get on the ball tomorrow and show him some headwork and good landings, I won't have to worry so much.

This evening I had my first hour of link trainer, and I came out with a "very satisfactory" grade. Those little things are really fun—they're just like a real plane. If you let the airspeed get down to the stalling point, you go into a real spin, and you use a genuine spin recovery like up in the air. All the sensations are practically like you experience when you're really flying—I really enjoyed it.

Also this afternoon, some of us St. Louis guys got some pictures taken for the St. Louis papers. You'll probably see them sooner or later.

This is Saturday night, but we don't get any open post this weekend, because we are behind schedule and they want to take advantage of the good flying weather. We might get off Monday night—I hope so. Another week of this without a break, and I'd be shot.

Here is the schedule I had today: There wasn't a breathing spell between any formation—reveille, breakfast, S.M.I. inspection, ground school (three hours), drill, noon mess, athletics, flying, link trainer, supper—and here I am with the room to polish up, lessons to get, and upperclassmen to ward off.

Tonight we were lucky—we didn't get any lectures. Practically every night a lieutenant gets the under class out in the circle at 8:00 P.M., and talks about discipline, inspections, etc., until 10:00 P.M. That is the only time we have to write letters or get lessons, so we're just out of luck when the lieutenant decides to lecture.

My books are calling, and I want to get through in a hurry so I'll be in the groove tomorrow; consequently, I'll end right here. Write soon.

Love to all,
Billy

I got in the bugle corps because it excused me from afternoon drill. I still had a pretty good lip from having played French horn in high school. I stood in the circle in front of the administration building to play "Tattoo" and "Taps." I played each call twice, facing different directions. "Tattoo" (ten minutes before "Taps") was my favorite. It allowed room for self-expression. Walking back to my barracks, I would sometimes hear compliments directed my way from cadets lying in their bunks in dark rooms. I appreciated a kind word in those days. For my bugling, I was promoted to cadet sergeant.

Dear Folks,

Things are looking a little better now. I still haven't soloed, but my instructor told me yesterday that my air work was all right, it is just the little things that I always forget that are holding me back. He's been a lot nicer lately, and I enjoy the dual rides a lot more.

I have $140.00 here, all ready to send home just as soon as I can get to a place where I can send a money order. The closest place is clear on the other side of Randolph, about forty-five minutes' walk from here, and I haven't been able to reach it yet, but I'll try to get it off this week.

We have a pretty classy drum and bugle corps here, and I got in it just for fun. I thought it would be fun playing a bugle with a bunch of other guys. Well, right off the bat they tell me to play the calls for Randolph Field tomorrow night. I'll have to play "Call to Quarters," "Tattoo," and "Taps." That should be something, putting Randolph Field to bed. I hope I don't ball it up as usual. If you folks were here to listen I know I would mess it up.

Well, this is Thursday evening, and I've put in another day of not-so-good flying. My instructor just took me up for about twenty minutes and gave me a forced landing. There was an auxiliary field nearby, but I didn't want to break into the pattern of that field, so I picked a nice long meadow a few miles away. Boy, that made him mad, and he really hopped on me. He said, "If your engine conked out over Randolph Field, I guess you'd hunt for a cornfield to land in!" Well, you can bet from now on I'll bust into anybody's pattern on a forced landing.

After we got down we had a little chat. He said, "Mitchell, do you have anything on your mind that worries you—any troubles of any kind?" I said no. Then he said, "Your flying is OK—you can handle the plane as well or better than the rest of my students, but sometimes you do the dumbest things! Do you know your left from your right? And when I tell you to lose altitude, why do you climb?" I told him that I had trouble hearing him sometimes, which is the truth. He gets mad and talks real fast, and I can't make out a word he's saying.

Tomorrow, he told me, we're going up for a long ride, and doing everything from spins to landings, and if I'm on the ball, I can stop worrying, but if I'm off the ball, I'll have lots to worry about. I think I'll make out OK, and if I'm lucky I'll solo. Here's hoping.

Boy, it's been hot lately, and these rooms aren't air-conditioned like the ones at Garner.

I'll seal this up now and get it in the mail. I have a lot of homework tonight, and it's all tough.

You all have been writing swell and I sure have enjoyed all the letters. I'll try to write more often myself.

Love to all,
Billy

I required more time to solo the BT-9 than I had needed to solo the PT-19 back in primary.

Dear Folks,

I have some good news tonight for a change! I soloed today! That's what I've been hoping and praying for, and it happened this morning. We went over to an auxiliary field and shot one landing, then my instructor climbed out and I made three solo landings. Boy, that really takes a load off my mind, because after one solos in basic, he's fairly certain of making the grade. It makes me feel pretty happy to look at one of those squat, heavy BT-9s and know that I can fly it all by my lonesome. I was beginning to get worried as you probably noticed in my letters, and I had good reason to, because I had nine hours before I did solo.

Nine hours isn't bad for a BT-9, though. If a guy shows enough promise they will allow him up to fifteen or twenty hours to solo. However, I wasn't showing much promise.

Last night I played the calls, and I'm still getting compliments. I really outdid myself, and I can't understand it. It isn't like me to come through under pressure like that. Maybe the worm has turned.

This is Saturday night, and the only reason I'm here on the post is because our Simon Legree navigation instructor gave us a pop quiz with a three-minute time limit and flunked three-quarters of the under class. We are confined to our rooms until further notice, and boy, that's hard to take.

I just wrote Bud a five-page letter and he'd better answer it or he will regret it. I spent one hour and a half on his letter.

Today while I was getting link-trainer instruction, the commander of the Gulf Coast Area Air Forces—Major General Harmon—came in and had his picture taken in a trainer right next to mine. I think that I got in the picture by craning my neck a little.

Those link trainers drive a guy crazy. We fly them for an hour every other day, and they tire me out more than a real plane. They sure are cute little things though—they would be fun to play around in.

I sure wish that you folks could come down while I'm at Randolph, because it is really a sight, and I'd like to show you around. Kelly and all the other advanced fields are pretty barren.

However, I would rather come home than have you come down here. Our commissions are drawing ever closer, and when and if I do get one, I'll most likely get a ten-day furlough along with it. I'm looking forward more to the furlough than the commission.

Also, if I wash out, I'll probably get a furlough. All the guys that have washed out so far have gotten lengthy furloughs, because classes in navigation and bombardiering were still in progress and they had to wait and get in with a new class.

I'll get some time off sooner or later, no matter what happens.

I guess I'll shower now, and then hit the hay. This confinement isn't bad in a way. I'll save some money and get some sleep.

Write soon.

Love to all,
Billy

The tone of the following letter indicates the pressure I was feeling. My instructor was not happy with the way I was flying. I had a minor accident on an auxiliary field at about this time. It was a fairly common and benign kind of accident known as a "ground loop." It happens after touchdown on a landing, when the pilot loses directional control of the airplane before the plane has slowed to taxiing speed. Wingtips are sometimes damaged in ground loops. My episode did not hurt the airplane, but it sure did not help my student-instructor relationship. I did not report the incident to my folks.

Dear Folks,

This is going to be a short one just to let you know that everything is going all right. I have about twenty minutes with nothing to do, and twenty spare minutes are pretty precious around here, so I'd better make the most of it.

We'll get our first cross-country about Saturday of this week, and we'll start night flying about next Tuesday, a week from yesterday. They're really rushing us through this place. It rained this morning and we might not be able to fly this afternoon. If we don't fly this afternoon, we will probably have to fly Sunday, and that would be bad.

I'm back from the flight line now, and we didn't fly—the field was too soggy. However, tomorrow I'll go up dual and fly under a hood using instruments for the first time.

Our flight commander of Hangar G is leaving us in a few days. He's a first lieutenant, and they're sending him to a four-engine school for a while, then he'll go over to some front. He is really happy.

All of these instructors down here would give anything to be on combat duty instead of the job they have, or any other job. They all signed up for combat duty, but not many of them get it right away.

The general idea is as follows: If you request pursuit aviation, they'll stick you in a bomber, and if you request combat service, they will put you in the ferry command or make an instructor out of you. You just can't win. I have to go to link trainer now.

Love to all,
Billy

Dear Folks,

Boy, if I ever do get through this place I'll figure that I can get through anything. I got off the ball again Saturday and didn't pass my twenty-hour check. My check pilot figured that my instructor was partly to blame, so I have another one now, but I regret it, because I was beginning to like my first instructor.

I went up with my new instructor today and gave him a fair ride. I did some things wrong and a few maneuvers right. We were scheduled for a cross-country, but a few clouds moved in and they called it off.

They're beginning to eliminate the stragglers now—they've gotten about six of our bunch so far, and there are a few others that are right on the verge—a little more so than I am. I think I'll make out all right—I made some crazy mistakes on my check that I'd never made before and won't again.

We had our regimental parade yesterday—the last one that Randolph will have, because they're taking our rifles away to give to the infantry. The parade ground was sprinkled with brass from colonels up to a major general, and our commanding officer told us that it was the best parade that he'd ever seen. The best part came after the parade. They announced over the PA system that the judges had decided that A Company (composed of us Uvaldites) was the best-drilled company on the field. There were about ten companies here, so we really did ourselves proud. Because of our A-1 rating, we won't have any inspections this week, and that's a real break for me, because I'm room orderly this week. Boy, you should've heard the yell we let out when we heard that we'd won. Everybody takes the parades to heart.

Well, I've got to sweat out three hours of ground school now, so I'll call it a letter.

> Love to all,
> Billy

I leveled out about six feet too high on one of my first night landings. The plane hit the ground so hard my goggles came unsnapped from my helmet and fell down around my neck. The BT-9 was ancient and approaching retirement, but it could still take punishment. The following letter is one of the longest I wrote as a cadet. It was written over two days and covers introduction to night flying, formation flying, instrument flying (under the hood), plus my report on a successful progress check ride.

Dear Folks,

Boy, I'm on the ball again, and I feel more confident about surviving this grind than I have since I've been here.

I told you I flunked my first check, didn't I? Well, three days later (yesterday) I took it over again and passed with a good grade. My check pilot told my new instructor that in the last three days I had improved 100 percent.

The check pilot gave me stalls, chandelles, lazy eights, eights down a road, and one power landing. The power landing was really funny. I never have been demonstrated one, and the one on my check was my first one, and I set it in perfect. It was the best feature in my ride, and the check pilot really laid it on thick. It's nice to hear some sweet words coming through those earphones instead of what I have been getting.

My new instructor is a first lieutenant—Lt. Hohenstein— he's a frozen-faced guy, and plenty tough, but he is a real pilot and I think he can teach me to fly—at least he has up to now.

I had my first instrument ride under the hood today. It wasn't bad. While I was on that instrument ride I noticed just how accustomed I am becoming to planes. The lieutenant flew me up to the altitude where I did my work and back down again, and it was just like riding in a car. I just sit back there and relax and think about everything else but flying. It's a lot different on a solo hop, though. You have to keep on the ball and think ahead of the plane then.

I shot a power approach stage today and it came out pretty good I think.

Last night we all had to go down to the flight line and inspect the planes. I put in a new battery with the able assistance of a sergeant mechanic. I found out something interesting about our BT-9s too. They used to be classed as pretty high-powered stuff, and instead of having dual controls with the instructor riding in back, a gunner was in the rear on a swivel seat with a .30-caliber machine gun. It feels pretty good to think that you're flying a combat ship. They still have all the machine guns here though, and I would give anything to take one up sometime and strafe some mesquite or something.

Ground school is my new nemesis. I flunked a navigation final a few days ago, and I'll have to take a re-exam. My code is OK—I can handle six words a minute now, and also my meteorology is in pretty good shape. That ground school really drags by. I really get sick of it.

The Boyds sound like nice people and I'd like to meet Miss Boyd with her car, but I might not have a chance to. We start night flying tomorrow night and it will be interfering with open posts from now till we graduate.

I almost forgot to tell you, in just a couple of days, maybe tomorrow, I'll start formation flying and buddy rides. Buddy rides consist of two cadets going up together and checking each other's instrument flying. That's what we guys have been waiting for ever since we started flying—a chance to see how the other fellows fly.

Thanks for the box—it goes good at night when I really get hungry.

I'll try to call Sunday, but don't expect it too much because I'll be confined to my room because of navigation.

Well, this is Sunday morning, and since I started this letter I've really had some diversified flying.

Saturday I flew formation for about an hour and it's really tough. The idea is to keep your eyes *always* on the lead ship— never look anyplace else, because the leader will clear the area and you don't have to worry about the planes. We made two formation landings and even then you can't watch the ground, you must glue your eyes on the leader and that's hard to do. We fly with our wingtips three feet apart and use the ordinary V formation and echelons to the left or right.

Last night I became a night flyer. I made three dual landings with my instructor, and then went up solo for an hour and shot four landings, which were pretty fair. This night flying is sure glamorous. There are all colors of lights on the field, and San Antonio really looks pretty. We use radios a lot at night and we land by floodlights.

We take off, fly to our assigned zone, climb up to the upper part of the zone, and circle around until we get instructions to drop to the middle part of the zone. Then we drop to the lower zone, and after circling there for a while we enter traffic and shoot four landings, then taxi on in and wait for the others to finish. There is a plane landing every minute, and we didn't finish until 2:30 this morning. That's a lot of landings.

Guess what! I'm a cadet sergeant now and I get to wear a mess of stripes on my arm. I'm also the new manager of the drum and bugle corps. But I'm not so tickled about that. Those sergeant's stripes are going to be nice though.

We'll be upperclassmen in a couple of days, and our dodos will probably come from Uvalde—the same bunch that we tormented there. I'm going to be pretty decent though, because I know how discouraged I got with all the hazing we took. I'll have to see that they all develop the Randolph shoulders back, chin in, chest out posture.

I'm going to try to call this afternoon about 1:30.

I wish that you could come down while I am still at Randolph, because it's so much prettier here than at the advanced schools.

My instructor is sure queer. When I'm up with him—for instance last night—he just screamed at me he'd get so mad. He'd call me a numbskull and everything, but when I got down from my solo ride and was sitting down in the grass watching the other planes land, he came up and sat down by me. He asked me if I had any trouble and if the plane was still intact, which it was. Then he said that he'd seen one of my landings and it was pretty smooth. He just smiled and got real chummy and it was hard to imagine that he was the same guy that had been calling me names an hour before.

Well, it's time for dinner now, so I'll start dressing and try to make it. This letter is late, but I hope the length will make up for it.

Love to all,
Billy

Another long letter follows. It amazes me today that I found time to write detailed reports when there was so little discretionary time. I mailed this one two days before my twentieth birthday.

Dear Folks,

What a grind! We're really working twenty-four hours a day now. Yesterday I took a cross-country down to a little landing field sitting way out in the middle of the mesquite about sixty miles south of here. It was a bad day for a cross-country. I had to alter my course several times each way to dodge local thunderstorms and such. When I did reach the field, it was raining hard there and I just turned around and came on back.

I had a lot of fun though. We have a swell system for locating ourselves when we are lost, and it is known as "buzzing a station." We find a little town on a railroad with a little brown depot and drop down to about fifty or a hundred feet and fly right by the station and see what town it is, then climb up and find the town on our maps. I buzzed a fair-sized town with a water tower that had the town's name on it. I dropped down real low and did pylon eights around the tower, and all the townspeople were out on the street gawking and cars stopped on the highway. It was fun putting on a show for the people.

Last night we flew again. I was up solo for an hour and fifteen minutes and shot four landings with landing lights (no floodlights). Those landing lights sure distort everything. We all made landings. We flew late again last night. I crawled in bed at 3:00 this morning.

Tonight, if we fly, we will go on a cross-country or else shoot blitz landings—landings with no lights—just a big black field to aim for. Neither one is much to look forward to.

I just passed my navigation exam. I think I got a good grade—in the nineties somewhere.

I tried to call Sunday, but I couldn't get you, and I had this navigation to study. So I gave up after an hour.

Daddy, I sure hope you can come down soon—I wish you could all make it, but I know how busy you are. I'll be counting on seeing you all when I get my wings at the Advanced Pursuit School at Victoria, Texas, in a few months. Boy, that's where I'd like to go. They fly classy planes, and their ground school consists of skeet shooting—nothing else. It's right down on the

Gulf, and the town had two dozen millionaires in it. (Have you
read about it in a recent issue of *Life*?). . . . I'm getting a little
ahead of myself though.

Dear Folks,

I'm sorry about this letter—it got held up because I just
didn't have time to finish it. Ever since last Saturday night,
we've been night flying, besides getting up at the regular time
and going through our usual schedule during the day. Since I
wrote you last, I've had two night cross-countries, and two
night *formation* cross-countries.

To give you an idea of how fast we're going through here, I'll
tell you about this formation stuff. I had about one and a half
hours of dual formation with my instructor sitting in the backseat, and I soloed in formation yesterday afternoon. Last night
I flew cross-country formation for three hours, so I had four
hours of formation yesterday. My eyes are so tired I can hardly
keep them open, and my arm that I use on the throttle is about
to fall off.

Day before yesterday I went on a 258-mile cross-country up
to Temple, Texas. When I went down to the flight line, my name
was last on the list to take off, so I didn't hurry about getting
my maps and data ready. About five minutes before the first guy
was supposed to take off, I looked up on the board and saw
that they had switched me to the head of the list, so I took off
without hardly any data except my maps, but I hit everything
right on the nose. A couple of the guys really got lost, but they
rounded them all up before dark.

The last two mornings I have been processing junior class-
men. I had about thirty-five men assigned to me, and I drilled
them for four hours straight each morning. I got more tired
than the dodos, and was plenty glad when it was over. I had
a bunch of Uvalde men that were our dodos there, so it was
more fun.

There are several St. Louis guys in the new bunch that came
down to Kelly with me and were put in cold storage down at
tent city while I was up on the hill. They were at primary with
Kenny Weir, and they said he made it OK, but he's going to
basic at San Angelo.

We just have two more hours of night flying to get, and

that's a big relief. I enjoy night flying, but getting four hours of sleep each night for a week isn't so hot.

This is Saturday, and I think I'll go into town tonight. I haven't been off the post for three weeks, and it's getting pretty old. I think I'll call up the Boyds, and maybe see them. Their number is in the phone book. Also, I'll call again Sunday and try to talk to you.

This formation flying is really fun. You'd be surprised at how easy it is to catch on to. We take off in formation, fly in formation, and land in formation, but the lead ship must always be a lieutenant—we cadets can't go up and fly a formation alone.

It's almost time for noon mess, so I'll try to get this mailed before mess. I'll write again Sunday and a lot next week, because we won't have to bother with night flying.

Write soon.

Love to all,
Billy

From the beginning of training, any time I looked ahead to an operational assignment in a combat theater, I envisioned the Pacific or Southeast Asia. In this letter I speculate that our flight commander "is getting us set for tactical duty in some jungle-infested place." As it turned out, I went to Europe.

Dear Folks,

Thanks a million for the swell box. That's the nicest package that's ever been received around here, and you should see how popular I am with everyone now. There's always a long line of guys outside my door just waiting for me to ask them in. The thing that went over biggest was the cake. One guy sampled a piece of it, and in three seconds it was all gone, so I just had to imagine how good it was.

Flying is purring along at the same old rate, except that now two cadets can go up together—one as an observer and pilot, and the other one under the hood trying to fly instruments. We have lots of fun doing that, and every once in a while we sneak in a chandelle or some other similar maneuver.

Two nights ago we made "blitz landings" with no lights at all. I landed the plane on thin air a couple of times and really jarred things up, but when you take things easy and feel the ground out, the landings are pretty soft.

They're really getting us set for tactical duty in some jungle-infested place, because our flight commander always gets reports and information from Burma, and Australia, etc., then we go out and practice landings in pint-sized areas, and blitz landings. Tomorrow we'll try to land on a little square piece of canvas out in the middle of the field.

We've been doing an awful lot of instrument flying lately—in fact that's about all I've been doing this week. Spins, stalls, and everything else under the hood. It's a funny feeling.

Ann Boyd wrote me a letter today, and I'm going to call them in the morning. She sounded very nice and offered to drive out here if I couldn't get off next weekend, but I think I'll be able to get off.

Cara, Dick has been carrying your letter around with him and reading it over again whenever he gets a five-minute break. He's all in a dither because he doesn't have a big picture to send you. He's sent them all away already. I wouldn't be surprised, though, if he doesn't get a new bunch made just for you. Right now he's out walking off five hours of tours for coming in three minutes after "Taps" from the post theater.

I am now living in a room with Gail Miller, George Merz, and Art Lynch. They are three swell guys and we really get along.

Well, it's time for a shower and some sleep now. Boy, it's nice not to have to fly at night.

Write often, and thanks again for the swell box.

Love to all,
Billy

As I explain in the following letter, "We're far enough along now so that we're beginning to worry about where we will go for advanced." Of course, I wanted to go to Foster Field at Victoria, Texas, where the ground school consisted of shooting skeet. The place to steer clear of was Brooks Field, right next door in San Antonio: where I went for advanced.

Dear Folks,

I wrote you a letter a few days ago, but I'm not sure that I mailed it. We moved just recently and everything got mixed up, and it might have gotten lost somewhere.

I spent today with the Boyds and had a swell time. I ate dinner out there, and Ann drove me all around town and showed me all the sights. After that we came back and sat around for a while then ate supper. Ann had a bunch of classmates from Texas U that were coming up to visit here from Corpus Christi. We went down to meet them at the station and one girl's father was a major and I met him and was in such a dither that I forgot to salute. I think Ann is a keen girl and we got along pretty well together.

They told me to come out next Sunday again and bring my three roommates also, which was sure nice of them.

My flying is shaping up pretty fast. I am all through with night flying, only lack one hour and a half of formation flying, and about eight hours of instrument.

I do my best flying in formation, for some reason. I don't have nearly as much trouble with it as with instrument rides and other phases of flying. Last Saturday another student and I went up in formation with my instructor and we dove in formation, sometimes exceeding 200 mph, and then we flew right through clouds in formation and we'd come out with our clothes and faces all wet from the water vapor in the cloud. My instructor would let us each lead the formation for a while, and he'd drop back to one wing position and fly so close that our wings overlapped about two feet. He is really a hot pilot, especially in formation and aerobatics. I just have another hour and a half to ride with him, and all the rest of my time here will be solo or with other cadets.

If instruments determine whether or not one goes to pursuit or bombardment, as in Bud's case, well, I won't have to worry about not getting pursuit. I am pretty sorry as an instrument flier, and I really hate to fly by instruments.

We're far enough along now so that we're beginning to worry about where we will go for advanced. Brooks Field is the place to steer clear of if possible. Some of our upperclassmen who went there say that it is as tough as they come, and they'd rather spend five days at Randolph than five hours at Brooks. They fly all day and all night and crowd in five hours of ground school some way every day.

I wrote a little bit down on the flight line this afternoon, and I'll enclose it too. Write soon, all of you, and give me the news.

I'm going to do some fancy sleeping now and try to catch up on what I've lost during the past few weeks.

Love to all,
Billy

Suddenly I became such a veteran pilot that I could philosophize about flying. It is a sign that my confidence is rising. There was good reason for more confidence. We had almost completed the second phase of the three-phase flight training program. Also, there was time to philosophize. The hard work in this phase was behind us. We were just putting in hours then. Flying was more relaxed.

Dear Folks,

This morning at 11:00 o'clock I had to take over the job of "charge of quarters" for twenty-four hours. I just sit in the CQ room here and fill out papers and answer telephone calls. It isn't hard, but it sure does interfere with my open post.

I had a date with Ann last night and we went to a show and then got something to eat. I had a nice time just riding in a car for a change. Airplanes are OK and practical enough, but you just can't beat a good car with four tires on it.

These buddy rides are really fun—that's about all we've been doing lately. I went up with Fred Moody yesterday for a couple of hours and we played around above the clouds doing a little of everything. I flew for one hour and Moody sat in back and kept me company. Then Moody flew and I sat in back and relaxed. The air was rougher than I've seen in a long time yesterday, and we got bounced around even as high as seven thousand feet where it's usually smooth as glass.

It's funny how flying can get in your blood and grow on you. When I first enlisted I didn't care a bit about flying—I didn't much care whether I flew or not. Throughout primary and the first part of basic it got monotonous and tiresome and wasn't anything but a lot of hard work, but during these past few weeks when we've been more or less on our own and what we do up in the air is entirely up to us, I've really begun to enjoy it. The idea of having so much power at your own disposal and so much space to zoom around in kind of fascinates me. My greatest desire now is the same as all the other guys. We would give anything to take a cross-country home and drop in at the local airport. That's what I dream about now—landing at Lambert

Field between a couple of Stratoliners or something on that order, and hopping out of the plane and walking up to the waiting room. Boy, what a commotion I'd create if I pulled in at Hastings with my 450-horsepower and eighty-mile-an-hour landing speed. I'd probably make a rough landing though, just when I wanted to make a good one. Also, I'd like to take Daddy up and do a snap roll or an Immelmann, except that I can't do an Immelmann, at least I couldn't worth a darn in primary, and we aren't supposed to do them here.

The main thing is that all of us cadets would like to show off a little. So far, our only observers have been veterans in this business, just itching to find fault with our flying. We'd like to take someone up that would get a thrill out of it. I'll have a chance to sooner or later.

Flying has permitted me to experience one unusual sensation—that of "blacking out." My instructor took me up once for the purpose of "blacking me out." We went into a spin, and came out doing about 200 mph, then he pulled the plane up into a vertical climb. It just felt like a black cloth was between me and the instrument panel. I couldn't see a thing, but I knew what was going on, and I knew where the stick and the throttle were, and I was fully conscious. It just lasted for one second, and there are no aftereffects at all. All of the fellows have blacked out at one time or another and everyone gets the same sensation.

It's almost dinnertime now, so I'll wind up this big letter. You've been writing pretty often and I sure like it. I've almost stopped writing everyone else, even Galloway.

Write soon everybody.

Love to all,
Billy

ADVANCED FLIGHT SCHOOL

Brooks Field, September to November, 1942

Moving from Randolph Field to Kelly Field "was like moving from a classy hotel to a boxcar." So said an aviation cadet in the 1930s. The same could be said in 1942 about moving from Randolph to Brooks Field. Both Kelly and Brooks Fields were veterans of World War I. A lot of aviation pioneering had taken place at both fields. Both looked threadbare after twenty-plus years of under-funded upkeep.

Cadets had started training at Brooks Field in 1918, just a year after Kelly became a flight school. Between 1919 and 1922, Brooks had been a school for balloonists. The balloon hangar was still there in 1942.

But Brooks had a redeeming feature for those of us who hoped to fly fighters. Assignment to Brooks meant that we had most likely gotten our wish. The airplane we would fly for our final seventy-five hours of training was the AT-6. This good-looking, sweet-flying advanced trainer, designed by North American Aviation, was the last step up the ladder to a fighter cockpit.

Two weeks passed since my last letter home. That was the longest interval between letters. A lot had been happening, including a hurricane, as I explain to my folks. The storm hit while I was still at Randolph. It came ashore around Corpus Christi and was still hurricane-strength when it reached San Antonio. I was in town when trees and telephone lines started coming down. Randolph's cadets were ordered back to the base where we fought the wind and rain for hours to hold down airplanes that would have otherwise flipped over or even cartwheeled

BROOKS FIELD, TEXAS

This illustration of AT-6 advanced trainers was the letterhead on the author's stationery at Brooks Field, Texas.

A Brooks Field AT-6 advanced trainer in its hangar, with an armed guard in the foreground. Courtesy The University of Texas Institute of Texan Cultures at San Antonio

away. We could lean almost forty-five degrees into the wind without falling over. It was an adventure.

Dear Folks,

I'm sorry that I've been so long in writing this. So much has been happening in the last week or two that I've been going in circles. I've written one already a few days ago, but I lost it when we moved.

We arrived here at Brooks Field this morning, and I don't know what to think of it. It's going to be the toughest grind yet—I know that much. We do a lot of flying and we're swamped with ground school—thirty-two different courses in eight weeks! Then, there'll be link trainer, calisthenics, drill, and all the usual stuff.

Brooks is supposed to turn out the best pilots in the United States—and I can see why, just by looking at the schedule. "Buzz" Wagner, Welch, and most of the other crackerjack combat aces graduated from Brooks, so I'll be following in some notable footsteps.

One thing has me worried though. I'm sure of my wings now, but I don't know what type of service I'll see. Graduates of Brooks become pursuit pilots, bomber pilots, and observation pilots—lots of observers. Observation is the one thing I don't want, so just watch me get it.

Anyway, we get pursuit training in big, single-engine advanced trainers and basic combat ships. We'll get aerial gunnery, lots of formation flying, and some dog fighting.

We had a big hurricane down here two weeks ago, seventy-mile-an-hour winds, torrential rains, and all the damage that you'd expect of a hurricane.

I was in town when it was blowing its hardest, and signs, trees, roofs, windows, etc., were toppling and blowing all over. Right at the height of the storm we all had to report out at Randolph to hold the planes down on the ground. They were practically taking off, and some blew over on their backs. It was really a sight and, boy, did we ever get wet. The damage amounted to a million dollars in San Antone alone, and down on the Gulf at Corpus Christi, Aransas Pass, Victoria, and Matagorda Island, the damage was terrible.

I sent a money order home, finally, and you should have it by now. I also have a lot of souvenirs—pictures of Randolph,

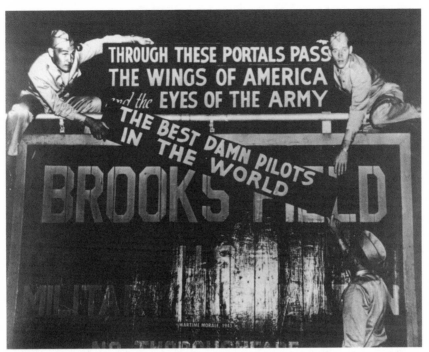

THROUGH THESE PORTALS PASS
THE WINGS OF AMERICA
and the EYES OF THE ARMY

THE BEST DAMN PILOTS IN THE WORLD

BROOKS FIELD

MILITA

Cadets attach an amendment to a sign over the entrance to the advanced flight school at Brooks Field, Texas. Photo courtesy The University of Texas Institute of Texan Cultures at San Antonio

annuals, cross-country maps, etc.—that I have all wrapped up ready to send. They were piling up on me and I thought that they'd be better taken care of at home than here.

During the last two days at Randolph we really concentrated on advanced acrobatics. Loops, Immelmanns, vertical snap rolls, vertical reversements, snap rolls on top of loops. My plane would get in some of the screwiest attitudes, and I wouldn't know just what was coming off. I was solo, so it didn't make any difference.

It's getting close to "Taps" time, so I'd better start getting a little sleep. I'll need it around this place. I'll write soon.

> Love to all,
> Billy

I was always dreaming. Of course, I did not know it then, but I would not get time off at graduation (much less get an AT-6 to fly to St. Louis). I would not get time off at Christmas, either. In fact, almost three years passed before I could get home on leave.

Dear Folks,

Today in navigation I figured how long it would take me to make St. Louis from here in an AT-6. I estimated about seven hours, including two stops for refueling. My first stop would be Dallas, and the next one Tulsa. Wish I could get a chance to try it someday. Maybe I will when I get commissioned.

I sure hope you folks can come down for graduation. I'd like for you to meet my instructor. He is absolutely the funniest guy I have ever seen; I can laugh just looking at him. He gets so worked up, and he talks with his hands a lot. I'm really crazy about him.

Boy, I dread becoming an upperclassman around here. Those poor guys go to ground school all morning, fly all afternoon, eat supper, then fly most of the night. They don't have any time off. They even miss out on most open posts. They're within smelling distance of their wings, so I guess they have a lot of incentive but, just the same, it's a grind that I'm not looking forward to.

Daddy, I couldn't tell you now whether or not I could get off or when. In another two weeks we'll start night flying and that will fill up my evenings, and our open posts are very indefinite. I'll probably get all day Saturday off this weekend. Then Saturday night and Sunday next weekend. Then Saturday off the next week. It alternates like that. If you could get down here some weekend, when I have Saturday night and Sunday off, it would be swell. I would like to have you come out to the field and look the planes and everything else over. I'm sure I could get you on the post. They aren't slipshod around here, like at Jefferson Barracks, about letting people in and out. There are hundreds of enlisted men walking around here with rifles with fixed bayonets, and they use them too. Every once in a while about midnight, I'll be woken up by a "Halt!" then another "Halt," then a rifle report, and then a lot of hot talking by the sentry and the guy who didn't halt.

We have been studying planes ever since we've been in the air corps, and we have access to all the government's restricted information on firepower, performance, speed, ceiling, and all the other specifications.

They don't compare at all with what you read in the papers. You probably never heard of the Heinkle He 113, and the North American P-51, but they're probably two of the best fighters in the world today. The Spitfire is right up there too.

The P-51 hasn't been mass-produced yet, but will be soon. Don't believe what you hear about the Messerschmitt 109, the Zero, the P-40, the P-39, and other headline makers. They are strictly second-line stuff, almost obsolete. Just wait till those P-51s and P-38s (another good one) fill the skies. They're the real death dealers.

Well, I'm not going to start another page. I didn't intend to write this much. But I can't seem to stop. I'm including a picture that might be interesting.

Write soon.

Love to all,
Billy

Two of my closest cousins were aviation cadets too. Reuben (Bud) Gentry, who was a year and a half older than me, was about two months ahead of me in flying school. At the time of this letter, Cousin Bud had just graduated and was assigned to fly the B-26 Martin Marauder medium bomber. The B-26 was the fastest and sexiest bomber in our inventory. Bud must have been considered an unusually promising young pilot to have been chosen to fly this airplane. Bud completed a combat tour in North Africa and returned home to be checked out in B-29s. The war ended before he had to see combat again.

Brooks (Brookie) Mitchell was a year younger than me, an experienced horseman and a crack shot. He had been captain of his rifle team at Highland Park High School in Dallas. Brooks and his father came to San Antonio to spend a day with me. This letter describes what a big time we had. Brooks became an aviation cadet soon after our visit. When he finished flight school, he was assigned to fly the F-51 fighter. A short time after his group arrived at their base in Italy, Brooks crashed and was killed when the oxygen system in his F-51 malfunctioned.

Dear Folks,

Boy, I had a wonderful time yesterday. Uncle Tom and Brookie were down here and I was with them from 11:00 A.M. until 9:30 P.M.—not much time, but we covered a lot.

Brookie is still having bad luck. His leg is OK, but last week a horse threw him down, and his arm is in a cast. Also, he just smashed up their new Buick and they don't have a car now.

Brookie isn't going to school—he is going to join the air corps—and to listen to him, that's final, but, of course, Uncle Tom says different.

A snapshot of author's cousin Brooks Mitchell standing on the wing of his PT-19A primary trainer.

Reuben (Bud) Gentry, the author's cousin, flying left wing in a formation of B-26 medium bombers en route to a target in the Mediterranean theater.

He came down here to ask me all about it, and I told him all the nice things about it, and the glamour of San Antonio sort of carried him away, and he's going to put in his application next week. He is crazy about the life we lead and our uniforms—in fact, I have never seen him more enthusiastic.

We rented a big blue convertible and Brookie and I cruised all around. I brought him out here and showed him the planes and everything. We really had a swell time all day.

This morning I got up dog tired and flew for four almost solid hours. Boy, I'm sure dragging now.

A norther blew in here last night and it was actually chilly this morning. We all wore leather jackets up in the planes and turned on our heaters.

I got lost this morning for the first time—I wasn't exactly lost, but I sure didn't know where my destination was. I was supposed to shoot landings at a little auxiliary field about twenty miles or so from here. There was a solid overcast at about fifteen hundred feet, so I found a tiny hole and went up alone in it—flew a course of 120 degrees for eight minutes, then dropped down through the overcast again, expecting to find the field, but it wasn't there. After circling around for a few minutes I just turned around and came back. I think my compass was off or something like that.

Have you gotten the souvenirs that I mailed last week some-time?

Daddy, I sure hope that you can make it down here soon. I guess I'll hear all about it over the phone tonight.

I hope you all can come down for my graduation, because it's a cinch that I won't get a furlough.

Well, it's time for me to trot over to a link trainer, and as much as I hate to, I guess I'd better.

I've been getting lots of letters lately from everybody and it sure is nice. Write when you have time and root those Cards on in for me.

Love to all,

Billy

I was doing a practice spin recovery when I messed up my sinuses. I had done two turns in the spin and then neutralized the controls. The airplane recovered nicely in a steep dive, as it was supposed to do. My mistake was that I let the plane stay in the dive too long. Airspeed got a little excessive, and when I pulled out of the dive, gravitational pressure probably aggravated my sinuses somehow. I had a cold, which did not help matters.

I did not feel anything at the time. Later that day, pain developed just above one eyebrow. It continued for several days, although I could control it somewhat with aspirin. Under no condition was I going to see a doctor. The possibility of getting washed out because of sinus trouble just weeks before graduation was not acceptable.

But the pain got worse. I suffered through a couple of nights with little sleep. The spot above my eyebrow—the pain center—swelled out into a marble-like shape that I could feel with my fingers. That scared me enough that I went to the hospital. The doctor treated me, as the following letter describes. The treatment worked and I was not washed out.

I do not recall the visit by Dad mentioned in the letter. It is possible he came when I was in the clutches of the sinus problem and was unaware of everything but the headache.

Dear Folks,

I'm just getting around to a letter. We've sure been busy lately.

Monday morning I didn't have a headache by 8:00 and we had a cross-country that was very important, so I went ahead and took it, and took some aspirins along with me. It didn't ache a bit on the trip and not even all day, but this morning I had one again, so I went to the hospital.

The doctor grounded me for a couple of days, and used a new machine on me. One attachment sprayed stuff up my nose and another one put a suction on it and about sucked my brains out of my nostrils. Then he gave me some pills and nose drops and told me to come back in a couple of days. It should fix it up.

Daddy, I think you'd be interested to know that last Sunday while you were here, President Roosevelt, Henry Wallace, and Stimson were out at Kelly Field looking the place over. It's the authentic truth, but the papers kept it completely quiet. They had a seventy-two-plane formation for him. Too bad we couldn't see him.

I'll write again tomorrow morning. I'm supposed to get a little sleep now and kill this cold.

Write soon.

Love to all,
Billy

The next month was hectic. There were social obligations, uniform fittings, graduation arrangements (Mom came down), catch-up hours in ground school—and we had just started night flying, which meant that we did not get to bed before 1:30 or 2:00 A.M. for two or three weeks.

Dear Folks,

This will be another short one. Just to let you know that everything is all right. I'm going over to the hospital this afternoon to try to get cleared for flying again. I'm sure they'll OK me.

I talked with my instructor this morning and he was sure swell. He said that he had sinus trouble himself and he knew how I felt, but I don't know for sure if I do have sinus trouble; anyway, whatever it was is OK now. If I do get cleared this afternoon, I'll fly tonight.

The way things look now, we'll graduate November 11th, and we'll have afternoons off for about a week before that, I imagine, so the 8th will be just about the right time to come down.

There are more parties on the fire for us when we finish up. There is the regular graduation dance, then the flight that has had the most accidents has to throw a party for the other flights, and, also, my instructor is giving a party for his students.

Friday afternoon—Last night (Thursday night) I night flew for the first time, and, boy, was it a mess. The ceiling dropped down to about twelve hundred feet and we were flying through scud half the time. I made thirteen landings—three dual and ten solo. I got in bed at 2:00 A.M.

Tonight we are scheduled for a three-hundred-mile cross-country, almost to Houston and back.

I am feeling fine again—no more headaches, thanks to the nose drops.

If my letters start petering out in the next few weeks, and they seem real short and a little further in between, don't worry, it's just that I'm so busy now that I can't write more than two paragraphs at one sitting.

We just heard that we won't fly tonight, because some bad weather is moving in, and everybody is running 'round with happy looks on their faces.

Well, I'm going to mail this along with some pictures Galloway sent me.

Write soon.

Love to all,
Billy

Just weeks until graduation, and the rumor mill was working three shifts. The first half of this letter deals with what is *actually* going on. The second half reports the hottest rumor.

Dear Folks,

I just came in from another cross-country. I missed out on one when I was grounded, so I made it up today. I was kind of on the spot, because there was a major in the backseat. He had to get a few hours in so he could get his flying pay, so I had to take him around. He told me to go ahead and fly like I was all alone, and not to worry about him. He climbed in, turned his seat around, propped his feet up on the gun mount, and went to sleep. But he woke up about halfway around and looked at the scenery. I made it pretty smoothly—thank goodness. He told me my navigation was good, when we got down, but he didn't care for the crow-hop in my landing.

There are millions of rumors circulating around this place. They are building lots of very long concrete runways to handle A-20s and P-51s, and P-40s, and that's what the rumors are all about. Some say that we are the last bunch of cadets to come through here, and it will become a tactical outfit. Others say that we'll start flying the aforementioned first-line airplanes as soon as the runways are completed and the ships brought in, which will be about November 20th. All these conflicting reports keep us going in circles.

Everything seems to be coming along OK. We're ahead of flying schedule; I'm Class I in ground school, and I don't have any more headaches.

I can hardly wait until the 8th. I hope you all can make it. Our upper class is graduating day after tomorrow morning, and we will fly a revue for them.

I'll tell you all about it.

Write soon.

Love to all,
Billy

I did not tell the folks about one adventure that took place about this time, in early September. I was solo, practicing acrobatics at seven thousand feet in a practice zone southeast of the field. The plane was inverted, halfway through a slow roll, when the engine quit. I called the tower and asked for instructions. They cleared the runway and told me to come on in.

It was a north-south runway, as I recall. I was to land south, so my landing approach had to be over downtown San Antonio. Of course, it was a "dead-stick" approach—I had no power. But I had about five thousand feet of runway to work with. So I landed long and fairly hot, and really greased it. I was thoroughly pleased with myself. Giving an "everything's under control" wave to the ambulance and fire truck that had come out to meet me—I hit the throttle, cleared the runway, and taxied back to the parking area. As I was taxiing, it dawned on me: The engine is running again. I have power. How will I explain this?

As I recall, an explanation was not needed. I answered a few questions, and that was it. I heard speculation that a saboteur was putting sugar in our gas tanks. That sounded to me like a theory cadets would hatch.

Dear Folks,

Well, finally we got a breathing spell and I can write a nice relaxed letter. We've really been working an eighteen- to twenty-hour day for the past ten days.

We took six cross-countries this week—all well over three hundred miles, and two of them at night.

Yesterday we flew down to Laredo, then once to Pawnee and back to Brooks. The country that we flew over would make the sandhills look civilized. There were absolutely no checkpoints—not even a cow. One guy made a forced landing out there, and he said, when he got back, that he wasn't worrying about being found, he just hoped that the Indians wouldn't get him.

Last night we ate a quick supper after returning from Laredo and took off again for Corpus Christi. I hit everything just right and really enjoyed it. It's a real thrill to head out into total darkness with your destination 150 miles away. That cockpit really feels cozy. We flew a light line down to Corpus and then cut right across open country to Yoakum, and then followed a light line back to Brooks.

We're taking an interesting course in combat aviation. Our instructor is a Captain Wenn, who flew a pursuit plane on the Western front and with Allenby in Palestine in the last war. He is a Scotsman and was in the RAF. He flew in combat from 1915 to 1918. In 1915 the enemy planes didn't even shoot at each other. Captain Wenn said that he would pass German planes, each going on observation missions, and they'd thumb their noses and go on. After a while they started equipping the observers in the rear cockpits with carbines and they'd take a few cracks at each other, and a few planes were actually downed with rifle fire.

Captain Wenn showed us some little steel darts that the World War I pilots used to shower down on enemy trenches. They'd get a handful of darts, dive down on a trench, and drop them over. It sure sounds primitive, but those darts are wicked-looking outfits.

It's almost a dead cinch that I'll get to fly a first-line pursuit plane eventually. If I get observation, I'll fly a souped-up speed demon, and if I get pursuit, naturally, I'll fly a pursuit plane. The thought of flying a stripped-down, souped-up P-38 and leaving Messerschmitts in my propwash intrigues me, but I want to cause some destruction even if I have to take along a pocketful of darts.

Nancy, how are you getting along? I don't hear very much from you. Do you still play baseball with the boys?

Well, time has passed in a hurry, and my ten-hour open post is drawing to a close, so I'd better shower and get to bed.

I can't find Mary Sasser's letter, so I won't enclose it, but I'm sending you my picture.

Note the results of not getting a haircut often enough, Daddy. It looks pretty shaggy.

That's the picture the papers will use when I get my fifth Jap. Good night.

Love to all,
Billy

I had grown up with guns. Hunting was a big deal in my family. Now I would be able to attack a target in an airplane armed with a machine gun. The prospect was too thrilling for words.

Dear Folks,

I'm realizing more each day just how wonderful sleep is. When I get an opportunity I'm going to experiment and see just how long I can sleep at one lick.

During the last four days I have flown two thousand miles of cross-country, both day and night; I still haven't gotten lost, but a lot of other fellows have. We take a night cross-country and the next morning our operations officers go all over Texas, rounding up guys that couldn't find their way home. It's fun to hear their stories.

Today we got a lecture on machine guns and tomorrow we'll start making practice dives on targets. I hope so.

My instructor flew up to Denver today. He's going to stay for three days and come back. I sure wish I could've stowed away. He said he could make it in six hours with two stops.

I think I'll stop now and do some serious sleeping.

Write when you can.

I feel fine and everything is ahead of schedule and running smoothly.

Write soon.

> Love to all,
> Billy

The following letter relays news from Cousin Bud and Cousin Brooks. It also makes clear that I am counting the days until graduation. Only eighteen or nineteen to go.

Dear Folks,

I hope you haven't been noticing the lack of letters from me too much. I slacked up a little lately, but with just one or two more nights of night flying left, I should do better.

Last night we took another cross-country, and one leg of it took us down to the Gulf. It was the first time I have ever flown by moonlight, and it was sure beautiful. The highways and rivers really shone, and the Gulf looked pretty good too.

Today we flew gunnery for three hours and I'm really tired out. I didn't get in until 1:30 last night, and after diving on targets all afternoon, I'm exhausted.

It's been very hot all day and I really got a sunburn this afternoon.

Good night, I almost forgot to tell you, Brookie is in the air corps. He passed his physical and mental and probably will be called in about three months.

He's really happy about it.

Bud is flying the hottest bomber we've got if he's flying the

B-26. They'll outrun a Zero, and they are the most beautiful planes that you can find—real streamlined.

Thanks a million for the swell box. It went over big all over the barracks. A couple of guys didn't even go to lunch—they just filled up on cookies and prunes. As soon as it came, I grabbed all the apples and locked them away.

The athletic instructor is having a commando obstacle course built for us. They're working on it right outside my window and I can see the thing taking shape. There is one big board wall that is about three times as high as I am, and I can't see how I'll get over it.

Boy, that old graduating time is drawing nigh. Just about eighteen or nineteen more days to wait. The time sure is creeping now. We've been counting the days for weeks now.

The graduating ceremony isn't too impressive—at least our upper class didn't have a very good one, but that doesn't make any difference to me.

Well, I think I'll go down and shave and shower. It was really dusty today. Thanks for all the letters.

Love to all,
Billy

The tailors delivered our officers' uniforms. We were a bunch of peacocks, fighting for the mirror. I advised Mom of a change in her hotel reservation, from the Gunter to the Plaza. I caught that mistake just in time! The Gunter was a party hotel on the weekends. At graduation, it would be a three-ring circus.

Dear Folks,

My letters are kind of few and far between lately, but there has been so much to do and take care of that I've had a hard time sitting still long enough to write.

Mom, when you come down you are to stay at the Plaza Hotel. I started thinking a little after we made the reservation at the Gunter, and I know that the Gunter will be a madhouse during graduation week—it always is anyway—and you probably wouldn't get any sleep, so I made a reservation at the Plaza, which is a nice quiet hotel. Can you tell me what time of the day you'll arrive—they'd like to know at the base.

Boy, I got my uniform today—all tailored and everything, and man, does it ever look neat. Just about everyone got theirs at the same time and they installed a new full-length mirror in our barracks just for us to parade in front of. We're really eager.

We've been doing a lot of formation flying lately, and we've done some things in formation that would've seemed impossible to me a few months ago. Lieutenant Forte will be leading, and all of a sudden he'll make a steep diving turn, or a chandelle, or lazy eight, and we blare right along beside him. Then he'll try to lose us. Boy, we'll dive until the plane vibrates all over, then pull out into a vertical climb, and then into a tight circle, or anything—throttle wide open all the time. He always keeps it at a good safe altitude and never tries to stall us out, but we really have some wild rides. On some of those dives and tight spirals I've actually had to brace my foot against the instrument panel and pull back on the stick with both hands. It really fags us out, but it's a lot of fun, and I bet it looks neat.

It looks like I'm going to be a bomber pilot. I'm about two inches too tall for pursuit, and I think I can evade observation. What I really want now is a single-engine dive-bomber or attack plane. Something like the Curtis "Hell Diver." They make them and test them out at Lambert.

Boy, this place is sure full of excitement now with graduation near and the question of where we're going and what we will fly always being discussed. I never heard so many rumors in my life.

The cooler weather has put an edge on my appetite and I've gained about five pounds in the last ten days. I weigh almost 150 now. I've been trying to stunt my growth for pursuit for quite a while, and since it looks hopeless now, I'll just go ahead and grow.

I hate to cut this short, but I can't neglect my ground school and still graduate, so I'd better get busy.

I wish you all could come down, but when I get commissioned it will be a lot easier for me to come up and see you, which I will do soon even if it is AWOL.

Write soon.

Love to all,
Billy

HELLO, SILVER WINGS, SO LONG, SAN ANTONE

Graduation for the Brooks Field contingent of Class 42-J was an afternoon event on November 10, 1942. We had not expected it to be a gala, and it was not.

The ceremony took place in one of the hangars. A small group of student pilots from the Netherlands graduated with us. Mom was there, and I believe we went back to the hotel for dinner.

That is all I remember of that day. Of course, if Mom had not been able to attend, I would have written a long letter home—a final letter from the pilot factory. It would have told the folks everything about the graduation address: the music (if there was music), and the thrill of becoming an officer and a qualified air corps pilot. But Mom was there to take it all in, so a letter was not needed.

FINAL REQUIREMENT: 50 HOURS IN AN O-52

Now we had our wings and lieutenant's bars, but before we left Brooks Field, we had one more assignment to handle. Artillery officers were learning to direct fire by air. We were to fly the planes they used to reach their target areas at nearby Camp Swift. It would take us about five weeks and fifty hours of flight time to complete this job.

The assignment would not be worth mention if it were not for the type of aircraft we flew. It was the Curtiss O-52, a 600-horsepower high-wing monoplane nicknamed the "Owl." The Owl was introduced in 1940 and was intended to fulfill a reconnaissance role. But the plane was deemed too slow for a combat theater, and only about two hundred

The author at graduation, November, 1942. He is wearing a uniform from the Sol Frank Company, San Antonio's longtime tailor of military finery.

had been built. They were used for sub patrol, courier duty, and other utility missions.

The O-52 was infamous for three reasons. First, it was a notorious ground-looper. That was because the landing gear retracted into the fuselage, which meant the wheels were too close together to provide much stability on the runway. Second, the landing gear was retracted manually by means of a hand crank in the cockpit. It took about fifty turns of the crank to get the wheels up, by which time the pilot was well on his way to wherever he was going. Third, the pilot was blind in a turn because he sat directly under the wing. To negotiate a turn, he had to drop the wing into his field of vision. He could not "look into a turn" as we had been taught to do from our first days in the air.

To get around this problem, Brooks Field had established an O-52 operating procedure that prohibited pilots from turning more than forty-five degrees without leveling out to clear the area. In other words, any turn had to be performed in forty-five-degree segments interspersed with straight-and-level visual checks. It was too bad that we had to say goodbye to San Antonio from the cockpit of this strange little airplane.

THE PLAYGROUND OF THE PILOT FACTORY

In 1942, going to San Antonio for the first time was like going to another country or continent. A young man from the Midwest, the Deep South, the Northeast, or the Northwest would be absolutely unprepared for what he found.

The city looked graceful and dignified despite the crowds and clamor of wartime. Seventeenth-century missions, standing here and there in residential and commercial neighborhoods, lent an atmosphere of timelessness. The heart of downtown was not the customary grid of streets. Instead, a meandering river, artistically landscaped, had the right of way.

City history rang with heroic names and shrines. The Alamo! What red-blooded American boy did not know (and believe) the story of the men who fought to the death in this citadel? Well, there it stood. You could walk right in like Davy Crockett did a hundred years before. And next to the Alamo stood the splendid old Menger Hotel, the headquarters of Colonel Teddy Roosevelt and his Rough Riders when they were organizing for the action that would lead them up San Juan Hill.

The young women of San Antonio were especially attractive. On warm spring Saturdays in 1942, they dressed up to watch soldiers, sailors, and cadets parade down Houston Street. Dark-eyed senoritas in white cotton dresses gave the crowd an exotic and exciting diversity. (At that time, more people of Mexican origin lived in San Antonio than lived in any city except Mexico City and Monterrey.) The relationship between the civilian community and the military in San Antonio seemed to me to be relaxed and well established (compared with what I would later see in other army towns). The city had been a military center for a long time. Kelly Field, Brooks Field, Randolph Field, and Fort Sam Houston were prestigious institutions. Old soldiers came back to retire in these friendly and familiar surroundings.

A cadet could grow up fast here in 1942. Young men who had not yet sampled the perks of adulthood or the pleasures of dissipation were ready to get on with it. San Antonio was prepared to accommodate.

Most of us were regular smokers, so the main unexplored issues were alcohol and women. I was slow to get around to both. I was so uncorrupted that a red-letter day was the day I discovered San Antonio's fruit juice stands. It was a balmy afternoon in March, my first day in town. At a juice stand in the heart of downtown I bought a glass of fresh or-

The San Antonio River looking downstream from St. Mary's Street Bridge.
Courtesy The University of Texas Institute of Texan Culture at San Antonio

ange juice for a dime or a quarter. Down the street at another stand I got a glass of fresh grapefruit juice for the same price. It turned out that there were juice stands all over town. There was nothing I liked better than fresh fruit, and, besides, I thought the juice would be good for my night vision. Since it was a great day to stroll, that is what I did, from one stand to another, all afternoon.

Two months later, in May, the Texas citrus season was over and the juice stands were gone. Then the highlight of a day off was a steak and a beer with my buddies at a restaurant on Houston Street. Good beer was cheap and plentiful in San Antonio. Two local breweries produced plenty of Pearl and Lone Star, which they had on draft and in bottles. The Pearl brewery had been there for more than sixty years. I did not know it then, but the cowboys who used to drive cattle through Indian Territory to markets in the north took Pearl beer with them, as long as it lasted. Teddy Roosevelt's Rough Riders drank Pearl. A cold Pearl suited me too in the early summer of 1942.

By July my libation of choice changed to rum and Coke. Mixed drinks were prohibited by law, as I recall. So the rum was brought to the table (or booth) in the paper sack that the liquor store provided. It was always a pint bottle, no matter if there were two at the table or four or six, and the brand invariably was Ron Rico. We would order Cokes and spike them. This was an indulgence popularized at the Cadet Club.

The club was on the mezzanine of the Gunter Hotel and was considered the appropriate place to meet a nice San Antonio girl. The dance floor was the center of activity, and a Saturday afternoon tea dance was the main event. Cadets who were good dancers did well at the Cadet Club. Liaisons that began on the dance floor sometimes (I heard tell) led to parties that ranged up and down the halls and in and out of guest rooms at the Gunter. The hotel was a happy hunting ground for cadets who were good on the dance floor and relaxed and confident around women.

The rest of us chased women in more repressed ways and in less productive places. Shyness was a problem for me and for others. Most of the kids who came to Texas with me were from towns, cities, and farms in Iowa and Missouri. We had come straight from homes where parents were in charge and where economic hard times exerted stern discipline on what we did with our time and money. Now, suddenly free from parental and hometown surveillance, and with cash in our pockets, we could really break out. We were ready to test our new freedoms, but we meant to do it in a more or less gentlemanly way. We could not forget that we would soon be commissioned officers and that the president would repose "special trust and confidence in the patriotism, valor, fidelity, and abilities" in each of us (or so the order read that would commission us as U.S. military officers, provided we did not wash out).

Those more experienced at picking up women did what they could to educate their backward buddies. Tips were offered, some helpful, some not. Such a teacher might even arrange a double date that would allow him to supervise on-the-job training.

No teacher, however, could discount the omnipresent fear of venereal disease. The thought of being washed out of pilot training because of syphilis or gonorrhea could splash cold water on the strongest biological urge. Fear of infection was reinforced by posters and lectures and especially by grim VD films shown at regular intervals in ground school. Military "pro stations" were strategically positioned in San Antonio neighborhoods where nighttime frolicking was common. These stations provided immediate prophylactic treatment to those who might have been exposed to venereal disease. The availability of the pro station may have stoked the carnal impulse in some. For me, the pro station was a reminder of the prevalence of disease. It was also a place where a reputable person would not want to be seen. (Would a visit to a pro station show up on your record?)

That is how I remember the San Antonio I discovered sixty years ago. Beautiful and exciting. And sensual in ways I was too cautious or too square to fully explore. Maybe it is just as well.

OUT OF THE FACTORY AND INTO A FUNK

December, 1942, to February, 1943

Between December, 1942, and February, 1943, I was assigned to the C-47 transition school at Del Valle Army Air Force Base in Austin, Texas. My letters do not make clear when I actually got the news that I would not be assigned to fly fighters. I probably passed that disappointment on to my folks by phone. It was a black day for me, that is for certain. I would have resigned myself to a light bomber, a medium bomber, or even a B-17. But a C-47? A Gooney Bird? I had never considered the possibility that I might serve out the war flying an unarmed plane. It was no consolation that a good share of my classmates were assigned to C-47s too. How would I announce this humiliation to my cousins Bud (who flew B-26s) and Brooks (who flew P-51s)?

The sad fact is that the air corps' requirement for C-47 pilots shot up dramatically just at the time I graduated. It was an unfortunate coincidence brought about by two decisions made at the highest level of Allied war planning. The first was the decision to create an airborne army to be used in the eventual invasion of Europe. The second was the decision to create a massive aerial delivery system to provide military supplies to China. This would lead to the establishment of the air route over the mountains from India to China that later became famous as "the Hump."

These two strategic commitments created an urgent need for C-47 pilots.

Of course, we newly graduated Brooks Field pilots did not know the strategic background to this turn of events. All we knew was that we

were single-engine pilots and that our future was supposed to be in a
fighter or a dive-bomber or (unlikely) a super-fast photo-recon aircraft.

I felt like I had washed out after all.

It did not help matters that this new Del Valle Army Air Base at
Austin was of tarpaper construction and that we had to walk from
building to building on wooden duckboards to stay out of the mud. Nor
did it help that Christmas was coming up.

Dear Folks,

This is another grind that we stepped into. Four hours of
ground school plus four hours of flying plus athletics and everything else that must be taken care of every day.

We're flying DC-3s, the biggest of the commercial airliners.
They're tremendous things and they fly like a freight car. They
give better than two thousand horsepower with a ninety-seven-
foot wingspan, and they can stay aloft for about ten hours or
better. I don't like them a bit—however, they are easy to fly.

Pilots on commercial airlines must have fifteen hundred
hours as copilot before they are checked out as first pilot. We
will be qualified first pilots in thirty hours. That's how fast we
have to absorb the stuff. I hate the thought of being stuck in
these things for the duration, but that's what's going to happen.
We can't transfer out.

Tomorrow night is Christmas Eve and all of your presents
should be there except Daddy's. It will probably be a day or two
late because the only decent men's store in town didn't stay
open late until tonight.

I didn't have much time to choose around among the stores,
so I tried to find something to please you and be easy to mail.
Some of the fellows will fly Christmas Day, and I don't know
for sure that I'm on the list. If I'm not and don't have to fly
Saturday, I'll run up to Dallas.

The CO told us we'd get a leave when our thirty days are up
here, which will be around January 20th. I think he meant it, so
you'll probably see me then, if not before. You never can tell
when I'll drop in at Lambert.

Well, I have a million things to study tonight and it's already
late, so I'd better get started.

Mom, would you mind sending me those two good pictures
of Gloria sometime? I'd like to see what she looks like again.

Merry Christmas everybody. I wish I could be there, but Bud, Wally, Uncle William, and a lot of other guys are in the same boat with me, so I can't gripe. I hope you like your presents.

Love to all,
Billy

The routine at the C-47 transition school resembled the cadet grind. The following letter is the first one I dated by day of the month. My previous letters had been dated with no more than the day of the week.

Saturday, January 2, 1943

Dear Folks,

It sure was swell to talk to everyone yesterday morning. Nancy, you sound like a young lady now.

The presents were swell and every one of them was exactly what I needed. I've been using that old billfold of Daddy's, and it's been falling apart gradually, and that one that Nancy sent was really the stuff. We have a lot of identification cards to carry, so all of those little cardholders will come in handy.

I never have any clean ties it seems like, and Cara's ties came when all of mine were wrinkled up, so I really made full use of them.

I'll see about the camera and try to get some good pictures as soon as possible.

I haven't read the book yet, but I think I can start it this weekend.

Boy, have we been busy! We work from 7 A.M. to 6 P.M. with forty-five minutes off for lunch. I've been shooting landings in their planes all week and I can really ease it down smoothly now. I was supposed to fly this morning, but I have more time than the other guys and they're going to let them catch up this morning.

I don't guess I told you about the record player I got while I was still at Brooks. We went down to pick out some records for Nancy and I was there all day, playing everything they had. They also had some neat portable Victrolas with a real nice tone, and before I realized it, I had bought one. I only have six records but I play them to death. Some of them were intended for Nancy, but I decided that she'd rather have some jewelry and I couldn't give up the records. I found Harry James's "Trumpet Rhapsody," and I'm making up for all the times I used to listen to MJB [a St. Louis disk jockey] in hopes that he'd play it, which he never did.

Our commanding officer had a talk with the Group CO, and the Group CO had some fresh reports on the troop-carrier command's activities in North Africa, and our CO told us about it a few days ago. I guess they do everything over there, from transporting parachutists to carrying mail. One crew member on a troop carrier set up a machine gun in the door and shot down three French pursuit planes that were heckling him. General Doolittle recently awarded sixty medals to pilots in the North African campaign, and forty-three medals went to pilots in the troop-carrier command.

George Merz and I were pretty low for a while, because we neither one wanted these things, but they might not be so bad after all. We can feel like we've qualified to fly about anything now—twin-engine or single-engine, and even four-engine, with a little more experience.

It sure is nice to know that the people I know back in Kirkwood are interested in how I'm doing. It makes a big difference.

Bud seems to be having a good time hedgehopping in his B-26. I'm going to write him today.

Well, time to eat, so goodbye for now.

Love to all,
Billy

My first "solo" in the C-47 with another student pilot brought much less a thrill than any previous solo. Two friends and I then found a duplex in town we could rent for $37.50 a month. The reason we needed off-the-base quarters is not clear from the following letter. Perhaps we had completed the time allotted for transition and needed to give up our quarters to a new class of student pilots.

January 13, 1943

Dear Folks,

Your letter came this afternoon and I'm going to answer right away for a change.

George, Moody, and I have found us some quarters in town. It's a duplex sort of a place with one twin and one single bed. It isn't ritzy or anything, but plenty nice for $37.50. We couldn't find an apartment or anything and we were almost set to rent a house when we found this duplex. It has an Electrolux refrigerator and an Electrolux vacuum cleaner, and Moody boasts that he can cook waffles, biscuits, or anything, so we're going to set up housekeeping. We'll either move in tomorrow or the next day. The address is 1005 West 28½ Street, Austin, Texas. You can address my mail to either my city address or the same old address. I'll be out here every day and can pick it up.

The furlough is still undecided; it will all depend on the disposition of the CO of my new outfit. Don't count on it though, because I don't have the least idea of what will happen.

About two days ago I soloed in one of these planes. Another student and I took it up alone. We had quite a hectic time because the radio went out and our landing gear retracting mechanism went on the blink. Everything worked out OK though, but in spite of the size of the ships, and all the mechanical failures that happened to us, I got less thrill out of that solo than any before. I guess I like the idea of a plane with a canopy that will slide back so that the breeze can blow around my ears, and I like to do my own flying without a copilot sitting next to me. These planes are the very best things in the world to fly as far as getting a world of experience in big ships is concerned, but it just doesn't seem like flying anymore, with that steering wheel in front of me, and the cockpit all enclosed and that big clumsy fuselage dragging along behind.

Sunday we took that long cross-country—fourteen hundred miles. I either flew or navigated all the way and, boy, was I fagged when we landed here. We ate lunch in Shreveport, Louisiana, instead of Fort Worth, so I didn't see Brookie. I found out beforehand where we were going to stop, so I didn't wire him or anything.

Sunday, while I was gone, Del Valle had an open house and fifty thousand people were here looking around, and another two thousand couldn't get in it was so crowded. The governor was out here. Del Valle rates around Austin, and everybody treats us well. It's really a swell town, a perfect contrast to San Antonio.

Moody's flying tonight. George is on his bed writing to his folks telling them of his engagement. (He went to Atlanta on a cross-country last Saturday and popped the question to his girl.

Mom, you mentioned that dreamy look in his eyes, well, you
should see them now!)
Hope to see you all within the next two weeks.
Love to all,
Billy

Fred Moody, George Merz, and I had been alphabetically linked since
we shared a barracks with a bunch of other M's and Mc's and Mac's at
pre-flight school. We became real buddies. Fred, from Taft, Texas, was
six years my senior, a courtly Southerner who was like a big brother.
George, from Jersey City, New Jersey, was two years older than I but
seemed more mature because he had served in the Army Air Corps in
Panama and Trinidad. He had been an engineer/gunner on a patrol
bomber and, according to a letter I wrote home from Uvalde, George's
bomber had sunk a Nazi sub near Aruba.

We had not learned it yet, but over time we would learn that the air
corps did not just take away your friends, it provided replacements too.

January 18, 1943

Dear Folks,
Well, I'm moving again—this time up to Lubbock, Texas.
The orders were a surprise to everyone, and nobody was ready
to go. I've been rushing around like a madman trying to get
everything straightened out. I'll leave this afternoon at 2:30.
Moody and Merz and I will be split up. Moody's staying
here to finish up some flying he missed out on when he was
sick. George is going to Sedalia, Missouri. And I'm going to
Lubbock.
George left last night and I told Moody goodbye this morning. Boy, was it tough. We ate together last night at the same
table in the same hotel where we always eat when in town. After about ten minutes we were all using handkerchiefs, and we
didn't give a hoot who saw us. Boy, I'm going to miss them.
My chances of a leave depend on the CO at Lubbock. I don't
know what he'll say, but don't count on it. I'm going to ask for
one as soon as I get there.
I have a Special Delivery letter out at the house, I found out
this morning, so I'll pick it up before I leave.
This has really been a mess the last two or three days. We
just got moved into the house when the special orders came,
and all of our baggage was mixed up. We had to get cleared

from Del Valle, and that's a day's work. We had to get transportation and a lot of other details.

I sure hope that I can get some time off when I get there. We sure are due for some leave.

I'll write again when I get there.

My address will be 61st Troop Carrier Group, Lubbock, Texas, as far as I know now.

Love to all,
Billy

IN SEARCH OF A SQUADRON

January to March, 1943

I left Austin by train at 2:30 P.M., January 20, with orders to join the 53d Troop Carrier Squadron in Lubbock, Texas. When I got to Lubbock, I discovered the squadron had just left. I caught up with the 53d in Stuttgart, Arkansas, where I joined it and spent the next five weeks as a copilot, sitting beside some relatively experienced first pilots, towing gliders and dropping paratroopers.

The squadron was part of the 61st Troop Carrier Group, one of the first organizations to be assigned the troop-carrier mission. These aircrews had been training together for months and were considered ready to be sent to a combat theater. I was one of a handful of newly graduated pilots assigned to the organization as extras. We were there to replace any copilots who needed replacing due to sickness or accident. Departure time for the overseas theater was fast approaching, and all slots had to be filled. I spent a month with the squadron, and a month after I left, the squadron took off for North Africa.

I never felt I belonged to the 53d Squadron. Not the way I had belonged to Class 42-J at Uvalde, Randolph, and Brooks. I was just a "temp" with the 53d. If somebody needed a copilot for a glider tow, a paratrooper drop, a trip to the maintenance depot, I was available. It turned out to be a valuable experience, however. I got to watch a number of experienced pilots handle the C-47 at night and in formation and with a glider in tow.

Train travel was the pits during World War II. Sometimes it was impossible to find an empty seat. I rode all of one night sitting on a case of empty Coke bottles. My butt wound up dimpled where the bottle tops left their imprint. The dimples were so deep that they felt more or less permanent. I could not see the effect, but it felt to the touch like a waffle iron. It took a long time to go away.

January 24, 1943

Dear Folks,

It was swell to hear from you. I hope you didn't worry any before I sent the telegram.

Dorothy Galloway just called and she told me that Bill Nelson's father died this morning. I feel sorry for Bill and the rest of the family, but I think he is plenty capable enough to keep things going. Mr. Nelson was really tops.

I guess that you've been wondering about how I ended up here in Arkansas. We got to Lubbock, spent the night, and then got orders to come here—rather, eight of us came here. I sneaked in and pulled a few strings so that I could be sent here. It's strictly glider towing here, although this squadron is a tactical unit and has been moving around getting experience in everything from paratrooper to cargo carrying.

This field is really an advanced glider school, but the Fifty-third Troop Carrier Squadron just moved in temporarily to learn how to haul gliders and to teach the glider pilots how to be hauled.

My situation is very much different now, in that I must be prepared to go overseas on twenty-four-hour notice. Our squadron commander told us that it may be six months. I hope it isn't too long or too soon.

I told him that I was from St. Louis and he said that I could probably get a plane and a three-day pass and go home, but that I'd have to wait for a while until I'd gotten in a little more time with this squadron.

They have about three basic trainers out here just for traveling purposes, and I could get a friend and be up there in two and a half hours.

I was in Oklahoma City for a day and saw the Cates [my cousin Frances and her family] and Mrs. Dunham [the landlady of the rooming house in which I lived as a freshman at the University of Oklahoma]. Tommy is growing like everything and is as quiet as a mouse, and Roscoe is having a hard time with the union. He can't get anyone to work in the cafeteria.

Mrs. Dunham didn't recognize me for a while, but when she did she really wanted to talk. Reid is working for an oil company in Okmulgee, and Ranson is still in medical school. The university looks deserted.

I guess I've been traveling for about five or six days, and I've spent two complete nights on the train, both without a berth, and three nights ago when we came into Little Rock I didn't sleep a wink, but I sure caught up last night and the night before.

Stuttgart is a nice little country town of about five thousand, right in the middle of the "rice belt." It sure was a break for me to be sent here.

I'll probably see you all soon and I'll keep you posted on all the happenings.

My address is 53d TC Sqd., AAF, Stuttgart, Arkansas.

Love to all,
Billy

A bad reaction to vaccination shots sent me to the hospital. I tried to leave too soon and had to be readmitted. In this letter, I attempt to put the best face possible on my assignment to C-47s and the troop-carrier mission, but, privately, I deplored the whole situation.

February 5, 1943

Dear Folks,

I guess I have a lot of explaining to do, and I imagine you've been wondering why I haven't written or anything.

We got a cholera and a typhus shot about four days ago and a few of us really felt them. I got sick the next day and Williams lugged me over to the hospital. It wasn't serious, of course, I just felt good and miserable—chills, fever, and then chills again and I couldn't eat.

While I was in the hospital I got a little cold and I was afraid that the doc would notice it and ground me for a week or so— a guy with a cold is sunk if a doctor finds out. They won't even let you get near a plane. I figured I'd better get out of the hospital as soon as possible or they would notice the cold. I guess I left too soon, because right after I talked to Nancy I got woozy again, probably from lack of food, and I was in the hospital before I knew it.

Well, I'm out now and I feel OK. I tried to call tonight but I couldn't do any good, so, since I have an exam to study on, I sent a wire. Then you called and I went over to the phone again and waited to get connections and finally gave up.

Our long-distance phone is over in the club, a long walk from here, and we can't go in without a blouse on, and my blouse is usually at the cleaners. It makes it sort of hard when the lines are busy, too, like they were tonight.

I don't know if it's wise to tell anyone about the plans, and future of the 53d, but I think I am allowed to tell my folks just general ideas and such.

We probably won't leave the States for several months, and our squadron commander said that he'd see to it that every man got five days at home before that happens.

In the meantime, the 53d is going to whip itself into fighting trim and try to live up to its reputation as the oldest, most experienced, and most rough-and-ready squadron in the troop-carrier command.

The 53d has carried paratroops and hauled gliders, carried cargo and ski troops, and participated in desert maneuvers, and it was the nucleus—the first squadron organized—in the troop carrier.

It's a swell squadron and it's small enough so that it seems like a big family. Everybody is chumming with everybody except the squadron commander, and he remains just aloof enough to keep our respect, which is right.

I still burn when a pursuit drops in here, or when I see pictures of guys painting trophy marks on the sides of their little fighters, but I'm feeling a little more happy about our big colossuses. Tonight a formation of our planes thundered over the roof at about twenty-five-feet altitude with signal lights flashing and throttles jazzing, and I stood in the door and tingled. It was really a sight.

We're going to get range practice with .45s and tommy guns and all night hikes and other courses to mold us into fierce customers.

My sickness put a crimp in my homecoming plans. I was hoping to fly a lot in a hurry and make a good show and then ask for a pass, but I got sick and we've had some nasty weather, so my flying time is low and I'll have to build it up some before I can make it.

Your box came a few days ago and it was really swell. The apples were good.

When I first got here I wrote everyone I've ever known, practically. I figured that I'd really start getting letters, but nobody writes—except Moody. I've gotten four letters from him.

I'll be sending some of my excess baggage home soon. I don't ever want to move again with as much as I had to worry about when I left Austin. Boy, I had luggage strewn from Lubbock to Stuttgart on that last trip, but everything finally arrived. Williams left a trunk sitting out beside the tracks in front of the Amarillo, Texas, depot without a check or anything. He finally got it though, after about a dozen telegrams.

I heard from Bill Nelson. He seems to be very cheery and I guess everything is OK. Thanks a lot for sending the flowers.

We are "rumor-ridden" around here. Some guys start them maliciously, and others think they have the real dope. The latest thing tonight, just passed on by the guys in the next room, is that the pilots of the 53d will be transferred to the ferry command. Another fresh one is that we will be assigned to test a new version of the flying fortress designed as a dive-bomber. Both are just outgrowths of someone's imagination. Rumor-mongering is a pastime here as it is everywhere else, wherever soldiers congregate.

Well, it's very late and I've told you everything there is to tell, so I guess I'll call it a letter. I'll write more often.

Love to all,

Billy

P.S. Enclosing an article from *Liberty*—maybe you saw it. It's not big but it is quite an achievement:

Stop-Watch Tactics

Allied and neutral countries were startled by the swift Nazi air invasion of Norway, the parachute and glider "surprise" at Crete, and the rapidity with which Japan spread out over the Pacific. But these Axis operations really paled when the Allies moved into North Africa.

Parachute and other troops were flown 1,500 miles nonstop from England to North Africa with perfect timing—an operation far more complex and daring than the Nazi invasion of Norway and Crete. The planes arrived in the battle area after a flight as long as halfway across the United States. The dropping of the troops had to be timed to the minute with the attacks made by bombers and fighters, and the paratroopers were bailing out while combat planes were clearing the skies and neutralizing ground opposition.

Credit goes to Army Air Forces' newest organizations, the Troop Carrier Command, and to the Parachute Battalions.

As a copilot, I helped deliver a C-47 from Stuttgart to San Antonio's Duncan Field for maintenance. We had to stay there for most of a week. The air traffic at Duncan Field was something to behold. Aircraft of all types from all the fighting fronts were coming and going. Sitting in the cockpits of these parked warplanes, it was easy for a greenhorn pilot like me to fantasize.

Gunter Hotel—Thursday evening

Dear Folks,

Right after I talked to you, Mom, Sunday morning, they told me that another guy and I were to take a plane down here to Duncan Field for repairs. There was already one down here being worked on and we were to fly it back Monday morning. Those were the plans; however, first one thing and then another slowed the mechanics up—they couldn't get parts, the oil lines sprung leaks, and finally just about an hour ago we were all set to pull out, because the test pilot had it up for a final check. But our hopes were in vain, because one engine cut out on him and he had to land with a single engine. It's either spark plug or magneto trouble now.

This other guy and I stay in town at night and run out to Duncan first thing in the morning and stay all day, sweating out our airplane.

Duncan Field is an aviator's paradise. Paul would be nuts about it. It's the biggest air depot in the world and planes from everywhere, including the fighting fronts, come in for repairs and engine changes.

This morning I stood out in front of operations and watched a P-40, a Flying Fort, a Vultee Vengeance, and Roscoe Turner's old trophy-winning racer land one behind the other in the space of about five minutes.

Every type of army plane is there in great numbers. I've personally sat in four different pursuits, a B-24 fresh from the

Aleutian Islands, and best of all, *Suzy Q*, the most famous plane of the war.

I know you've heard about it, because it's been written up everywhere. I even talked to the first pilot, Lieutenant Colonel Hardison, and advised him about hotel facilities in San Antonio.

The *Suzy Q* has been all over the Pacific theater and has twenty-six little Jap circles on her side to indicate the number of Zeroes that thought they could, but couldn't. There are also eight question marks for the probables.

An RCAF flier came in today in a P-40 with seven swastikas on his plane. He got them in North Africa.

I've been running around Duncan Field in my leather jacket and with circles under my eyes, so for all they know I'm probably some hot pilot from the fighting front, just biding my time till they get my "peashooter" overhauled, so I can get back.

We brought down a captain from Stuttgart who was formerly publicity agent for Interstate Theaters, which includes every big theater in San Antone and practically every one in Texas, and he is really treating us right. We can go to any movie free, and he even got us a couple of swell dates. I really liked my date a lot. She works in an office out at Duncan.

I got Nancy's presents the other day down in a novelty store in the Plaza Hotel. I hope you like it, Nancy; it's different and I was a little doubtful at first. I was going to get you some more turquoise stuff, but that's all I've been giving you for such a long time, and a big box of these things would give your room a sort of Mexican atmosphere.

Well, it's time for supper now. If things work out OK, and if they get these women mechanics off our ship, we'll be in Stuttgart tomorrow.

You should hear my fellow pilot talk. He's from North Carolina and you could cut his drawl with a knife. These Texans sound like Yankees beside him.

Well, write soon, and I hope I can see you soon.

Love to all,
Billy

The new base I was sent to was Pope Field at Fayetteville, North Carolina. This was the home of the 82d Airborne Division, and I got my first glimpse of the paratroopers I would be working with for the next two months. I was impressed.

Saturday afternoon

Dear Folks,

Sorry that I haven't written sooner; I won't waste any time on explanation, because I think I'll be able to explain in person, maybe next weekend.

Down here we'll fly all week, and the on the weekends we can use 50 percent of the planes for personal cross-countries up to a thousand miles. I'm planning to come up next weekend with a fellow from Rolla if we can get a real experienced pilot to come along with us, and I think we can. If I don't happen to make it this weekend, I'll see you on one of the following week-ends, because we'll be here for about two months. I'll wire you as soon as I know for sure.

We moved in a hurry again—this time the whole squadron. I just climbed out of the plane from San Antone when they told me to start packing and settling all personal affairs.

We flew all the ships down in one big formation and I was in the lead ship with Captain Betts, the C.O. I had to navigate the whole bunch down here—725 miles without a beam or radio aid of any kind. We flew down at ninety-five hundred feet and there were layers upon layers of clouds under us, so I couldn't see, which made it really tough. I really didn't know for sure where we were 'til we hit Charlotte, North Carolina, but some wonderful guiding hand kept my plane on course and pointed my finger at the right place on the map when the captain wanted to know where we were.

Boy, did we ever say farewell to Stuttgart in style. Captain Betts is very young and has a flair for glamour and audacious-ness, etc., so our whole formation, twelve planes, buzzed right over the post and the city, clearing everything by inches. We ac-tually climbed to clear fences. I sure wish that we could buzz 129 Idlewild and Stanford University like that.

We're hauling paratroops about 50 percent of the time down here. You should see those guys—rugged! And they're the sharpest and the cockiest guys you can imagine.

We take them out here about twenty miles and drop them in a big field. They put their chutes on a truck and walk back in formation with full packs. As soon as they get back they take a few jaunts around their obstacle course, which is full of ditches filled with barbed wire and some really tough obstacles. When they're in town they're immaculate. Their para-boots are shined and their para-wings are polished, their clothes always pressed and they're always walking in a brace, shoulders back and chests out, like they wouldn't take any back-talk from anybody. And the paratroop officers—man, I met three of them yesterday and it was like shaking hands with Dempsey, John L. Sullivan, and Joe Lewis. They're really tough.

There is a red-hot division of paratroops stationed here—all ready to go across, and I really feel sorry for whoever or whatever gets in their way.

Associating with those guys has made the 53d a little physique-conscious and we run around all the time and try to get in shape so they won't think we're pantywaists.

We're really roughing it here—no orderlies and no elaborate messhall. We stoke our own stoves, rummage through the pinewoods for firewood, and eat GI food in a little shed. When we've gotta go, we run up a big hill to the Chic Sale. I'm in favor of it, because we were getting far too soft. Pilots are notoriously the puniest guys in the army, but I don't care to be myself.

We're tacked right on to the edge of Fort Bragg and it's the biggest thing you ever saw. We're always getting lost. Fayetteville is the town that everyone spends Saturday night in, but I don't care for it after seeing it just once. Too many soldiers and the same kinds of hijackers that follow the army around.

I was wondering if Charlotte Williams still goes to Duke. If she does, I might pay her a visit sometime, if I can get up there.

Well, the fire's almost out, so I guess I'd better go haul some coal in, and I haven't made my bed yet either. If I'm home next weekend I'll show you how a good cadet makes beds.

I'm flying four hours tonight. They must think I'm an owl.

Hope to see you all very soon.

Love to all,

Billy

P.S. I'm including a snapshot and an article from the *Tiger Cub*. The snapshot was taken at Stuttgart—the only snow I've seen this year.

SQUADRON FOUND

Alliance Army Air Base, March 15
to August 24, 1943

I n late February I said goodbye to the 53d Squadron. They were going overseas and no longer needed me or the other fledgling copilots
who had been made available in case substitutions were required. In
April the 53d (and the rest of the 61st Group) flew off to French Morocco. I would see them again at a reunion party in England in 1944.

We left-behind temps were given orders to join other troop-carrier
units in various stages of organization or training. My new assignment
was to the 73d Squadron of the 434th Troop Carrier Group, a brand-
new organization just being formed at an air base near Alliance in north-
western Nebraska. Getting there required another marathon train ride.
Fortunately, the trip took me through St. Louis and allowed a few days'
visit with my family in suburban Kirkwood.

Getting the 73d assignment was a good break for me all the way
around. To begin with, Nebraska was home country. I had lived in Hastings, Nebraska, from 1932 to 1940. My best friends still lived there.

In addition, I was getting in on the ground floor of the 73d Squadron. I was not part of the official "cadre" (a military term applied to the
core group of people around which a new unit is formed), but I was one
of the earliest of the early birds. This meant that I would have seniority
advantages and advancement opportunities not available to those who
came later.

The air crews of the 73d Squadron would fly together for about two
and a half years. Cohesion lasting this long was unusual in the air corps.
In most cases, individuals—not organizations—were rotated in and out
of combat theaters. Knowing each other for as long and as well as we

would was especially beneficial to the 73d's pilots, because virtually wherever we flew, day and night, we flew in formation.

On the March morning that I arrived in Alliance, the air was crisp, the sky blue, and the sun just warm enough to be felt. I had bacon and eggs at a café in town and found a taxi driver who would take me to the air base. I was looking forward to whatever the 73d had in store.

At full strength the squadron was to have at least thirteen aircraft and crews of its own. But in March, 1943, full strength was still several months away. Through the month we shared two C-47s with three other squadrons in the 434th Group. Our turn came every other day, and we owned the plane for just half the day.

Flying time was so precious, it was strictly rationed and supervised in order to provide training benefit to as many as possible.

Dear Folks,

Arrived here safe and sound yesterday. Everything worked out all right on the train. I reached Alliance at about 10:30 A.M. and came on out here to the field. I was all signed in and had a squadron assignment by 3:00. My squadron, the 73d, is brand-new, in fact our whole group, the 434, just came into existence. We have two airplanes for the group and the 73d gets one plane every other afternoon!

I was immediately made assistant communications and assistant operations officer, and in addition, I have to lecture on "interior guard duty" to a class of enlisted men on Monday and Tuesday.

Our CO is a captain and flew for Eastern Airlines. I will probably be checked out as a first pilot as soon as I've made a couple of landings with him.

The weather up here is wonderful, almost balmy. A few days ago it was twenty-eight below.

Alliance is a swell town and I think that I'll be very satisfied here. I got a jeep yesterday and went into town and got all of my baggage.

Our barracks are the best yet and although we burn coal, everything is kept clean.

The first person I ran into when I got here was Herbie Ritter, and I guess I'm going out to visit him and his wife this weekend sometime. Yesterday morning on the train I must've seen a hundred pheasants. They were walking around the fields like chickens.

That myth about southern hospitality and friendliness is just a come-on for tourists as far as I can see. I think I'll take old barren Nebraska over any state now. It sure is good to be back.

Our field elevation is 3,862 feet here, as compared with the 500 at San Antonio, 750 at Stuttgart, and about 300 at Pope.

Daddy, I'm sorry that I forgot about your birthday. I remembered before I left Pope, but I thought it was the 10th for some reason. When I got to St. Louis I never thought about it until someone mentioned it. I'll send you and Mom a package as soon as I can get into town during shopping hours.

Nancy, I hijacked a bunch of your records, but I left a few in return. I hope you don't mind.

We've got a good gym here with a punching bag, so I guess I'll start getting back in shape. We also have skeet shooting and a pistol range, and I have arranged with an enlisted man who is an ex-secret service man to get me some shells for my pistol, so I'll have plenty of recreation if I have time for it.

Write soon and I'll answer pronto.

Love to all,
Billy

I quickly began to reap the benefits of being on the ground floor in a new organization. I was made a "limited" first pilot, that is, I would not be fully qualified until I got my instrument rating. I expected I was in line to become a flight commander as soon as we got more airplanes and pilots.

Dear Folks,

It was swell to hear from you and I'm glad that you liked your presents.

I like this place better every day, and in spite of the fact that we just have two planes for four squadrons, I'm getting my share of flying.

Last weekend I went down to Austin and stayed over Saturday night. It was a pretty nice trip.

I haven't ridden with a first pilot since I've been here. They send me up with these boys fresh from Del Valle and I try to teach them a few things I learned in the 53d, so my title is now limited first pilot. I won't be unlimited until I get my instrument rating.

I think I'm slated to be a flight commander in our squadron, which is a swell job. A flight commander is supposed to be a captain, but it will be quite some time before it comes through. My silver bars aren't even in sight yet.

I flew over the Black Hills this morning just messing around. They sure look pretty.

It sure was swell to be home. I haven't gotten over it yet.

Boy, am I working. I drill the squadron, give them calisthenics, lecture to them on everything, usually something I don't know anything about, plus flying, and some classes that I have to attend. It's a full day, but this good Nebraska atmosphere keeps us going.

Well, it's very late and my light is keeping everyone awake, so I'll close for tonight.

Write soon.

Love to all,
Billy

We shared the base with two regiments of the 82d Airborne Division. They were the 326th Glider Infantry and the 507th Parachute Infantry. We would later work with these units after we had more airplanes and had logged more flying time. For the time being, they provided us with good models of the soldierly bearing and physical fitness that we had more or less neglected since we graduated from the cadet routine.

Dear Folks,

It's been hot as the dickens here today and I've got a good burn to show for being out in the sun all day.

I just finished a tour as officer of the day. Twenty-four hours buzzing all over in a jeep inspecting the guard and such as that, I must've put a hundred miles on that jeep. The OD carries a pistol always, so I substituted my Colt for the regular .45. They were short on pistols anyway.

We're still not doing much flying because of the shortage of planes, however, our group has set up a regular shuttle trip to Sedalia, Missouri, from here. There will be a plane leaving here for Sedalia every day. The 73d takes it every fourth day.

I'll have that allotment taken out of the next check I get if I

C-47s from Alliance Army Air Force Base fly a ragged practice formation over Mount Rushmore in South Dakota. Photo courtesy the Knight Museum, Alliance, Nebraska

ever get another one. Our personnel section is all mixed up and it's hard to get any money at all.

We have a whole bunch of paratroopers and airborne infantry here and they are tough like all the rest. We've been getting dirty-fighting instructions from the airborne guys over in the gym, and they've taught us some pretty good stuff. A real hand-to-hand tussle with no holds barred and all the science of jujitsu and cruelty of dirty fighting involved can get really savage. We just learn holds and escapes in the course.

There's a swell article in the April *Reader's Digest* entitled "Queens Die Proudly," all about the 19th Bombardment Squadron and the first few months of the war.

I guess Bud will be in the thick of it soon, if not already. I hope that we run into each other over there sometime.

I'm beginning to get pretty sleepy, and even if it is just 7:30. I think I'll go to sleep and catch up a little. Write soon.

Love to all,
Billy

Three officers and a noncom of the 507th Parachute Infantry Regiment at Alliance, Nebraska. The author felt that airborne soldiers such as these men were the elite of the armed forces. Photo courtesy the Knight Museum, Alliance, Nebraska

P.S. A guy on *Dr. IQ* [a radio show] just hit the biography question on the first clue. Seventy-two silver dollars!!

Fred Pierce, from McAllen, Texas, was my new roommate and close friend. He came to Alliance from the 53d Squadron at Pope Field at the same time that I did, but I did not know him before Alliance.

My following letter refers to a thoughtful deed of Fred's. He was returning to Alliance from a flight somewhere. He had been passing through St. Louis and had my parents' address, and he went out of his way to pay them a visit. What a surprise to them, and to me, too. They called me during his visit. The "Joe" mentioned in the first sentence is Fred.

Fred's nickname was "Little Dog," a name I believe he chose for himself to express his irreverence for "Big Dogs," or persons of high rank. Fred had a friendly swagger. He was fun to be around. As he was assigned to the 74th Squadron, we never got to fly together, but we roomed together the whole time we were at Alliance.

Dear Folks,

Just talked to you all and "Joe." It sure was a nice surprise.

Pierce is one guy I've really wanted you all to meet. He is the little guy I've been telling you so much about. You really can't appreciate him unless you see him bluffing his way around a bunch of men. He talks like he's trying to pick a fight, but he's never had a fight in his life.

I've been sitting here thinking about what all he could've told you. I can't think of anything that's too bad.

Our squadron has four brand-new planes now, which is about right for the amount of pilots we have, but we'll have thirteen planes when we reach full strength. This other group that's stationed up here, the 403rd, is joining the group from Sedalia on maneuvers. They're dropping paratroops and gliders all around these parts. Today they annihilated Kearney and McCook and rendezvoused over Harvard.

I got a letter from Moody today. He's down at Sedalia and would've been up here on maneuvers except he's stuck out in California on a cross-country. I'll be able to see him on that shuttle run that we've just started. He said that he had met Susan Hayward, the actress, and talked to her for at least an hour.

It's funny the way friends can get so spread out in the air corps. I always meet someone I've known before whenever I take a trip.

Here at Alliance I met a guy I hazed at Uvalde and another guy that just pulled into Uvalde when I left for Randolph. Then there was Ritter and several others that went clear through with me. When the Sedalia bunch came up, I sat in on a briefing they had just before takeoff time, and the guy in back of me pulled my ear and I looked back and there was Kenny Weir. He's rooming with Moody at Sedalia. There were a bunch of guys in that bunch that were at Brooks, Raldolph, and Uvalde with me. It's fun to meet old bay buddies like that, and they always have news about other guys.

Well, it's about time for a shower or something, so I'd better close.

I hope you folks liked Pierce. I really think a lot of him. Write soon.

Love to all,
Billy

Captain Dowling, our squadron commander, was colorful. He had been a barnstormer before he joined an airline, and he liked to tell stories about his barnstorming days. One of his stories described an act that the barnstormers publicized before their show, with great success.

The act featured a certain "Billy and His Death-Defying Leap from an Airplane at 1,000 Feet without a Parachute." Billy, it turned out, was a big rooster who, when tossed out of the plane, would fall head first like a rock until he was a hundred feet or so above ground, then he would spread his wings and flare out to a perfect landing. Billy's reward was a hen waiting for him in a pen at the landing site.

Dear Folks,

I'm sitting down here in operations now, waiting for 7:30 to roll around so I can night fly.

I said last night that my instrument card might be in my pocket soon. Captain Dowling, my CO, has been preaching instruments to me day and night. That's all I fly in the plane anymore, and he chases me down to the link trainers whenever I'm not flying. Today he went down with me and he practically revised the whole link-training system of the Army Air Forces. He's an old airline pilot with six thousand hours, and he's very emphatic and tempestuous, and when he wants to tell somebody something he waves his arms and bellows and acts like a wild man. Something this morning irritated him and he didn't think the link operators were doing it right, so he really raised Cain. My operator was so scared he couldn't talk. Everything was in a turmoil when I climbed into the link, and the good captain was standing right outside ready to jump on me for any mistakes. Boy, I was sweating!

I had to climb up to twenty-five hundred feet before starting the problem, and I was thinking just about the problem and studying my charts, and my airspeed dropped off to ninety and I went into a spin. The captain didn't say anything, and I went ahead and worked the best problem I ever have worked, which was, incidentally, an instrument orientation, approach, and letdown over Presque Isle Airport, the same place that Mrs. Davis's sister's husband embarked from.

We had a real thick dust storm today, but it's stopped now.

I spent last weekend in Denver again. I sure like that town;

it's so clean and pretty and interesting after a week or so out here in "Little Siberia."

Link trainers and women are making an old man of me.

Well, it's time to soar around a little bit, so good night for tonight.

Love to all,
Billy

The following letter describes a foolish indulgence called "buzzing." To buzz was to fly at extremely low altitude—to hedgehop, in other words. It was dangerous but authorized in scheduled training situations because in a combat theater, we would be safest from enemy ground fire when we hedgehopped. But it was fun to buzz. It was about the only exciting thing one could do in a C-47. And we did a lot of unauthorized buzzing. Here, I tell how I alerted my best friend Bill Nelson in my old hometown of Hastings, just a short flight away from Alliance, and then buzzed him and the whole city of fifteen thousand.

Friday night

Dear Folks,

I've been a flying fool this week—all night and all day. The first part of the week I was the only first pilot here, and we have about fifteen brand-new copilots clamoring for time, so I had to ride with them, and we were on a night schedule, so it was really rough. Monday night I flew for eight hours solid, just stopping to pick up a new copilot, and we were shooting landings all that time—about one every eight minutes.

About Wednesday night I began to wise up, so instead of driving myself nuts with landings I filed a clearance to Grand Island about five A.M., flew down there, landed, and called up Nelson and told him to be expecting me over his roof in a few minutes. Boy, I really buzzed that place. Nelson was standing out in the street waving for all he was worth. It was sure a thrill. Boy, the town looked pretty. I buzzed them again at 4:00 A.M. this morning but couldn't see anyone I knew.

I put in for a leave about three days ago and just heard today that my CO had approved it and it's now waiting on group's approval. It's to begin on the 14th, and I applied for twelve days, but if it is OK'ed it will probably be cut to seven or eight.

More news—we have a new CO. Dowling was transferred and his successor seems to be very nice.

Dowling and I never did get along worth a darn. We were always friends and all that, but we weren't very chummy. He pulled one last fast one that made me awfully mad for a while. We have two superb apple polishers in our squadron—both former artillery officers who went through flight training in grade. They graduated in 43-A, two classes after me.

They know the army from stem to stern, but as pilots they're worse than mediocre. They went with Dowling on all of his weekend trips and stayed as close to him as possible all the time. Just before Dowling left, he gave both of these guys an instrument rating while on one of these trips.

It sort of hurt my pride, because I have better than a hundred hours more than either of them and though I'm no HP, they are a lot farther from the "hot pilot" bracket than I am. Dowling never even gave me a whack at an instrument check before he left—in fact, I've only flown with him once, and we were towing a glider then. Pierce, who is darned good, took an instrument check under his CO and didn't make it, because of some little infinitesimal error. He's mad too.

Today I had some gratification, because one of these guys with the silver tongue had to copilot for me on a formation flight. The guy hadn't ever flown formation in these planes before and he's an unlimited pilot. This is just another one of life's little tragedies, I guess.

This is Sunday and I'm still a flying fool—that's why I can't finish a letter in one sitting.

Just about got to fly down to Hastings and spend the night. I had a ship, a crew, and a long passenger list, and my bag was all packed, then all at once the major decided that the ship should spend the weekend here for fellows to fly that weren't going on trips, and Grand Island reported a four-hundred-foot ceiling and closed their field—everything was against me.

Today I kept up my pace in the air—seven and a half hours—I either made or supervised sixty-five landings today and OK'ed two fellows to fly in the pattern as first pilots. Also made a trip to Mount Rushmore again and one to Cheyenne.

Pierce flew up to Winnipeg, Canada, today and I've been listening to his tales all evening and smoking English cigarettes. He got a steak up there for fifty-five cents, and people wanted his autograph and everything. He's been overflowing with stories.

Pierce and I have been racing to see who can get the most hours, and he's been telling me how I'll sweat when I'm on leave—if—just thinking about him piling up the hours. He said that he was in a nervous sweat when he was on leave, thinking how he was losing out.

Ceiling zero tonight, so I've just been playing records, talking, and writing.

If my leave is approved I'll be home either Saturday or Sunday (13th or the 14th), but the amount of leave is undecided.

It makes no difference to me where we go, just so there's plenty of food and a bed. If we go to Minnesota, let's stop at some lake toward the southern part of the state. This cold weather is getting old. Here it is June and we're still wearing coats and gloves and standing around stoves.

Well, time to turn the light out. Write soon, everybody. I hope I'll see you Saturday.

Love to all,
Billy

The so-called navigational training flight was the most popular perk offered by the 73d. A qualified pilot and crew could fly a plane to the city of their choice, remain overnight, and chalk it up to navigational training. They even got paid for it—a six-dollar per diem for time spent away from home base. There were some distance limits. And an airplane had to be available for a trip assignment. But on most weekends, airplanes were available, and crews would pack their B-4 bags late Saturday afternoon and fly as far away from Alliance as time allowed.

There were other opportunities to fly the coop when airplanes had to be picked up and delivered.

As this letter explains, I passed up trip opportunities in order to save money.

April 22, 1943

Dear Folks,

I had a chance to spend tonight in either Denver or Oklahoma City but decided not to in keeping with my new penny-pinching plan. Cross-countries are very expensive.

Yesterday we heard about the way Japan treats captive aviators. I don't know how other army posts reacted, but our whole base—air corps, paratroop infantry, and glider infantry—was confined to the post indefinitely. There's a Jap concentration camp fairly close by, somewhere in Wyoming, and there might have been some trouble. Now, more than ever, I wish that I could cause some death and destruction in this war—especially over Japan. Some people have been arguing against fanning hatred against our enemies, but I don't see how anyone can see Japan admit those executions without hoping for a chance to repay them with plenty of blood and thunder.

I'm practically an instructor now. We have a flock of new pilots from Del Valle and we're teaching them to fly these planes like the Fifty-third taught me. Boy, that time with the Fifty-third really helped, even if I did just have a copilot's rating. There is so much to learn about this ship that it's hard to believe, and those ace pilots in the Fifty-third gave me a good start. I'm still just a novice, but I'm learning while teaching.

Well, I'll sign off for now but will try to write soon and a lot more often.

Love to all,
Billy

My program of passing up trips and staying home in order to save money lasted two days.

April 24, 1943

Dear Folks,

I'm now known as Flight Commander Mitchell, and my silver bars should be here soon. The job calls for a captaincy, but I won't make that for eight or nine months yet. Pierce is also a flight commander.

That trip down to Fort Benning really was a reunion with my old buddies. On the way back, we stopped in Kansas City, and I was in a cafeteria. I looked up and there was Moody. He was in KC for one night and so was I, and we just happened to be in the same place at the same time.

We took a fifteen-mile hike day before yesterday with full packs and were strafed with flour sacks and gassed with tear gas all the way. Planes would come over just above the telephone poles and we'd sprawl in ditches while they rained down the so-called bombs. It was a lot of fun, but the footwork was killing, and we also dug foxholes and slit trenches when we made camp.

I was in Denver this last weekend and had a very good time. Saw Tommy Dorsey and he was supposed to come here, but couldn't make it for some reason or another. He wasn't very good anyway.

I passed over Hastings coming back from Benning, but there were twenty-eight passengers plus baggage, so I was powerless to do what I would've liked to. We maintained six thousand feet.

Was in my first thunderstorm yesterday. I got ice, hail, dust rain, and everything. All the other planes were in except me, and the tower was screaming at me to land immediately, but every time I'd come in for a landing, they'd designate a new runway to land on. I made three passes at the field before the wind was constant long enough for me to land without having too bad a crosswind. I had four passengers and they all got sick and tossed their cookies all over the floor.

It's time to eat now, so I'll close.

Please write soon, and I'll try to call tonight.

Love to all,
Billy

Here is a headline that appeared in the *Daily Oklahoman* newspaper, Oklahoma City, May 9, 1943:

Air Transport Crash Kills 14
on East Reno
Injured Army Man Near Death;
Plane Caught Fire in the Air

The plane crashed at about 9:30 A.M. on May 8, shortly after it cleared the runway at the Tinker Field Air Depot on a return flight to Alliance, Nebraska. The injured man died. The newspaper said it was the worst air disaster in Oklahoma history.

The airplane was a C-47 that belonged to the 73d Squadron. Most of the people who had been on board were members of the squadron. None of them was a close friend of mine, but the first pilot, I remember, was one of the most experienced pilots in the squadron. He was a first lieutenant from Atlanta.

Our squadron commander assigned a number of us to go to Oklahoma City in order to escort the caskets from the funeral home to the homes of the next of kin. I was assigned to escort the remains of our squadron communications officer. The funeral home coordinator told me emphatically to prevent survivors from opening the casket if at all possible. He told me, too, to establish which car in the train would carry the casket and to make sure that car was still part of my train when we reached the destination.

The young second lieutenant whose remains I escorted had lived in Richmond Hill, New York, which turned out to be in the vicinity of Brooklyn. There was an impressive funeral procession down Flatbush Avenue. I walked behind an ornate hearse. Following that, there was a military service at Mitchel Field.

After the services, an uncle of the deceased took charge of me. He drove me to my hotel in Manhattan and then escorted me to several big-name nightclubs, one of which was Jack Dempsey's. At each club the uncle told the man in charge to give me anything I asked for, then he told me good night and left. I had never seen hospitality to equal what I was shown in the city that I had always imagined would be insensitive, even hostile.

Quite a lot had happened since my last letter: the crash in Oklahoma City, my solemn trip to New York City, and a stop at home on the way back to Nebraska.

The tone of this letter says that everything is OK.

McLester Hotel
Tuscaloosa, Alabama
May 25, 1943

Dear Folks,

Just a quick note from a different town.

I'm in the process of ferrying a plane from Mobile up to Fort Wayne, Indiana, and stopped over here for the night. I'm first pilot, too, which is something new for such a long trip. They mostly require unlimited pilots.

Tuscaloosa is the home of Alabama University, but it's a very small uninteresting place.

We've been out walking around the town not doing a darned thing.

I landed at a primary school here and gave the cadets a thrill. I had to buzz the field in order to check the wind tee. We'll leave at 9:30 in the morning for Fort Wayne, so I'd better hit the hay.

I hope my leave will materialize about June 12, or sometime around then.

Will write more later.

Love to all,
Billy

Whoever came up with the idea for the Hotel De Gink deserves a medal. There was a De Gink available at many of the U.S. air bases where there was a lot of transient pilot traffic. The De Gink described in this letter was at Lowry Field in Denver. The point of the De Ginks was to make the transient feel like a real guest instead of just another traveler to be trundled off to a bed in the BOQ (Bachelor Officers' Quarters). This point was made by providing the little personal touches that a traveler would otherwise expect to find in a decent hotel of that time. For example, the following letter was written on Hotel De Gink stationery.

Officers' Mess, Hotel De Gink
Lowry Field
Denver, Colorado
May 28, 1943

Dear Folks,

Here I am at Denver again. Seems like I'm not in Alliance long enough anymore to even get my clothes cleaned.

I got back from that ferrying trip yesterday afternoon. The jaunt from Tuscaloosa to Fort Wayne was nice and smooth. I know I must've gone right over Sparta, but I was flying without any maps and didn't know just where it was in reference to Birmingham and Nashville. This morning I came down to operations about 8:30 and was told that I had to fly a guy down here to Denver immediately. This fellow had just had a heart attack and was in bad shape. They had him strapped on a stretcher in the plane already, and as soon as I filed a clearance we took off.

Since he was in such a bad condition, I couldn't fly at any altitude, so I hedgehopped all the way down, right over the housetops. I was supposed to go back this evening, but there are a lot of things to be overhauled on the plane, so we're staying overnight and leaving at 6:00 A.M.

Thompson is my copilot and we're lounging around in the Hotel De Gink, which is a place—very nice—for transient pilots to stay on the post. I'm just marking time till six o'clock when I can call my little Denver gal friend and see what she's doing.

You should've seen us cut up down at Tuscaloosa. Lieutenant Freeman had a bunch of friends down there and they came out to watch us take off. We got permission from the CO to buzz the field, and gave primary trainers a red light while we came over at five feet—Freeman first and then me. Boy, it was fun.

This Hotel De Gink is really nice. They have a De Gink at all the big depots. We have a nice room, soft beds, towels, soap, radio, lamps, and everything for one dollar.

The only drawback is the fact that I don't have any clean clothes and will have to see Miss —— in my work clothes, but that's all right I guess.

About time for a shower now, so until tomorrow or maybe day after tomorrow, goodbye.

Love to all,
Billy

We were flying night and day in order to qualify new men to become first pilots. One of the new pilots, Les Hultquist, was from Hastings, Nebraska, my old hometown. Les and I buzzed Hastings to a fare-thee-well one afternoon. But our most unforgettable flight together came before that, shortly after Les joined the squadron.

It was right after lunch break. I got in the left seat of the same airplane I had been flying all morning, I did a sloppy mini-check of the cockpit and, as a consequence, took off unaware that the rudder trim tab had been cranked hard left. Of course, the airplane did not want to fly right. It wanted to bear hard left, take out the control tower, and then corkscrew into the ground. Trying to prevent that from happening (but totally ignorant of what was causing the problem), I stood on the right rudder pedal with all my weight and hugged the yoke into my chest, barely able to keep the airplane flying. Meanwhile, Les—bless him!— kept his head, scrutinized the control pedestal, spotted the errant rudder trim control, neutralized it, and saved our lives.

June 15, 1943

Dear Folks,

I'm enjoying a sixty-minute breathing spell, so will write you and tell you how things are coming.

We're very busy and are practically up to full strength. I've been playing the role of a ferry pilot, instructor, test pilot, and whatnot.

Every morning we must be present at a medical lecture at

seven thirty. Flying begins at 9:00 A.M. and we have an hour break at noon for lunch. We fly all afternoon, and after dinner we pick up where we left off in the afternoon, flying till 1:00 A.M. or later.

This afternoon we had a wild formation flight for about three hours. It was just one long buzz—every farmhouse, hamlet, and train, and even ducks on the lakes, when there wasn't anything else. Talking about ducks, I got one last week with a little .30 carbine—on the wing too. We had about eight paratroopers' carbines and thirty rounds of ammunition apiece and we really declared war on the ducks. Mine was the only one killed though.

There's a new pilot in my flight now from Hastings. Les Hultquist is his name. I knew him, but not very well. I'm flying with him tonight from 8:00 till 1:00.

The squadron is taking shape now and is beginning to look pretty good. There is a swell bunch of fellows in it and it's fun even when we're working so hard.

My leave won't have to wait much longer I don't believe, because we're checking out a lot of new pilots that can help shoulder the load and I can slip out without anyone missing me. I went down to Denver again last weekend and had a pretty good time riding roller coasters, etc. Coming back we were in a formation—three ships—and had to thread our way through dozens of local thunderstorms.

Well, time's up. Will write more later.

Love to all,
Billy

Bull sessions now dealt with questions about when we would be going overseas. We were up to strength and far enough along in training to be doing some serious speculating about our departure date. One of the guys had it on good authority that we would finish our training "right up to the final phases" here in Alliance instead of having to move to another base.

Wednesday night

Dear Folks,

Flew eight hours yesterday and last night and made twenty-five "blackout" landings last night—no lights.

A "feather merchant" is a civilian. You are all "feather merchants."

Here's some more pretty important news. We will get all of
our training right up to the final phases here instead of moving
to some other field like we've been anticipating any day. I'm
glad, because the other field more than likely would've been
Pope Field.

Haven't been taking any trips lately. It's all been sweating
out landings with the new boys. We have enough planes and
pilots now for me to start organizing our flights. I have a good
bunch of guys.

I should have my silver bars very soon. Promotions were
frozen for about a month while they set up a new promotion
system. But it's all set up now and my promotion is in, so all I
have to do is wait.

I think I'll hit the hay tonight early. There's no night flying
because they're shining up the ships for an inspection by a
general tomorrow. I'll wear a tin hat, .45, leggings, and no tie.
Hot stuff!!

> Love to all,
> Billy

I was flying as much as eight hours a day. Even though my promotion
to first lieutenant had come through, I was in a sour mood. This letter
introduces "Smitty" (Kenneth E. Smith), a St. Louisan who would have
become a flier, war or no war. Smitty had attended Parks Air College
and had read how-to books by famous aviators. He would eventually
become our squadron commander. As I believe everyone in the squadron would have agreed, Smitty was the best pilot in the 73d and possibly the whole group.

> July 17, 1943

Dear Folks,

We've been flying too much really. The big dogs even figure
that we can subsist on one meal a day, so we miss out on breakfast and lunch and fly.

Right now I don't really care if I ever see another airplane
again, but I guess I'll be in the same old cockpit all day
tomorrow.

Smitty and I were just about to spend the night in St. Louis,
but at the last minute (thirty minutes before takeoff time) our
cross-country was canceled. I never was so disappointed. After
that defeat we decided to leave at 4:00 A.M. tomorrow morning

and spend Sunday in St. Louis, but group slapped a five-hundred-mile limitation on our trips, so we hit a brick wall again as St. Louis is better than seven hundred miles from here.

That week at home was really swell, but it spoiled me. I hate this hole now, and all I can think about is ways and means to get back home again. Everybody commented on how healthy and clean I looked when I came back. Now, however, I've assumed the old Alliance droop to my shoulders and bloodshot eyes and filthy clothes.

Today I drew my brand new .45 and a shoulder holster. It's a classy outfit and it's all mine, but I can't hit a thing with the pistol. Shot forty rounds at a tremendous target at about twenty-five feet this afternoon and could only find three bullet holes, and they were at least sixteen feet away from the bull's-eye. I'm going to depend on my .22 for Hun shooting.

We also got our navigators. We have four assigned to the 73d.

Now that I outrank Pierce I have managed to keep a semblance of order in our room. I make him mop up the room, make my bed, and shine my shoes, and if he dares to get familiar and even think that lieutenants are lieutenants, whether first or second, I put him in a brace in the corner.

Smitty and I are planning on taking next weekend off and spending it at home, group or no group, so you'll probably see me. Eight hours a day in a plane leaves one mighty run down, even just for a week, but the medics and the pilots are the only ones that realize it, so we'll just have to ignore group for a few days. Will write more later.

Love to all,
Billy

The four-hour limit mentioned in the following letter did not apply to cross-country flights, as I explain. The limitation on flight time was a sensible step to take. We were flying too much to no good purpose. I suspect the powers-that-be were in a hurry for us to pile up enough flight hours in order to be eligible to go overseas.

This letter introduces Jack Miser, who, like Smitty, would become one of my closest friends. Jack was from Columbus, Ohio, and had played basketball at Ohio State. He could not have been more than five feet nine inches tall. On the court, his balance and grace must have made up for his lack of height.

When Smitty married his sweetheart from St. Louis in September, Jack and I were best man and maid of honor. I don't remember who was which.

July 21, 1943

Dear Folks,

The laundry came today—thanks a lot.

We all got a break the other day—an order was published stating that a pilot couldn't fly over four hours a day except on cross-countries, so we'll have a chance to do a few other things. The day before, I had towed gliders for eight and a half hours and was about ready to go over the hill.

Jack Miser is on leave now and there's no telling when he'll be back.

Smitty and I intend to come down to St. Louis this weekend some way. I don't know if I'll be allowed to leave, or how we'll get down there, but we're both pretty set on it and will do our best.

I think I get an instrument check sometime soon now that I'll have a chance to practice a little instrument flying. I flew a link this morning and the operator turned off my airspeed, then my vertical climb indicator. I was just wallowing around without any idea of how my plane was situated, but I didn't spin, so he took out a wrench and unscrewed something, and my left wing went down and I thought I'd never stop spinning. He never did tell me just what was the big idea.

That's about all the news for the present. I hope to see you all again this weekend.

Love to all,
Billy

July 22, 1943

Dear Folks,

Here's some more evidence of what a man can do when he only has to fly four hours per day. Boy, it sure seems wonderful.

Of course, there are other things to do—code practice, classes, physical training, etc., but they aren't nearly so tiresome and don't require so much concentration.

I finished my four hours this A.M.—flew instruments and practiced single engine landings.

We had a terrific thunderstorm last night that started right after I finished towing gliders and kept up till dawn. Pierce and I sat up most of the night comforting each other whenever the lightning would be a "near miss."

The possibilities of my coming down to St. Louis this weekend are still about the same. It's hard to tell now, and as usual I probably won't know until the last minute. Smitty went to Fort Wayne yesterday and didn't get back until late last night, so I haven't seen him yet today to talk it over.

I guess I'd better amble on down to operations and make my presence known, so I won't seem to be too much of a goldbrick.

Will write more later.

Love to all,
Billy

We were doing a lot of flying in really big formations. In the following letter I make an insensitive reference to a tragedy that had just occurred in St. Louis. One of the CG-4A gliders being produced in a St. Louis factory had been towed aloft on a demonstration flight. It was part of a big armed forces celebratory event. On board the glider were the mayor of St. Louis, the president of the chamber of commerce, and other dignitaries. At an altitude of several thousand feet, the glider's wing broke apart, the glider plunged to the ground, and all aboard were killed.

As I mentioned in my letter, I had met the pilot of the doomed glider just a week or so earlier. He was one of the aces in the glider program. I met him at Stout Field (or Baer Field) in Indiana. He was there to check out an experimental lighting system designed to identify a glider landing zone at night. I had flown in from Alliance that afternoon. We had a short briefing, and as soon as it was dark, I took the glider pilot in tow for two landing approaches. I had the impression that the glider pilot was pleased with the lighting system. It was probably about 9:30 P.M. when I finished the second tow and headed back to Alliance.

August 3, 1943

Dear Folks,

Nothing unusual has happened—of course, we're growing hotter and more ready by the day, but the day of departure is still a guess.

Just got back from a big maneuver down to Sedalia—forty-four-ship formation down and back, and, boy, was it work.

The papers tell me that one of our gliders sort of cleaned out the St. Louis city hall. The glider pilot that was killed was the same guy that I towed down at Indianapolis just before my leave—he was a darned nice fellow.

We had a big revue last Friday with our wing commander in the reviewing stand. It was a unique revue and really a thrill. We had all the planes lined up on the ramp and each crew was lined up in front of its plane with side arms, tommy guns, carbines, etc. After the inspection we took off and went into a mass formation. The wing commander had his reviewing stand right out in the middle of a runway, so we aimed our formation at him and gave the old crates full needle. Our group CO had told us to bring the formation in as low as possible, just so we didn't get any sod, so I brought my flight right down the runway, below the level of the reviewing stand, at 200 mph. The colonel was right in the midst of a big salute to the 73d when we came up to the stand and, boy, did he and his staff scramble when we came over. They liked it though, and I thought my heart was going to pound a hole in my side. That formation that we saw down at Lambert was really mild compared to this—thirty-six planes in formation five feet off the ground buzzing the old colonel.

I'll try again to come down this weekend—right now the prospects are fairly bright, but you know how much faith one can put in prospects up here. I couldn't say for sure until three minutes before takeoff time.

Will write more soon.

Love,

Billy

A lot of news is packed into the following letter, my last one from Alliance and, it appears, the last I wrote home while still in the States. (There may have been letters after this one that were not preserved.)

Getting approved for instrument flying was important, especially for me, because I much preferred to fly by the seat of my pants. According to a definition coined by a naval aviator, "Instrument flying is when your mind gets a grip on the idea that there is vision beyond sight." It made sense to me that a pilot must be able to maneuver the airplane without referring to anything outside the cockpit. I could do it. But "flying a beam" and other aspects of ground-controlled approaches were, for me, the most difficult lessons to learn.

The dedication ceremony that I mention in this letter still amazes me. An estimated fifty-nine thousand people packed into that isolated ranch town to see it! In the whole state of Nebraska, only Omaha and possibly Lincoln had populations that big.

The mock airborne attack was a popular demonstration. We had successfully mock-attacked several cities in the state when the decision was made to stage a mock invasion of Denver. The drop zone was Lowry Field. At that mile-high altitude, the air was thin, and the paratroopers dropped like rocks, many landing on runways and taxiways. We heard there was a high incidence of broken legs and ankles.

The bivouac in the Black Hills did not live up to my prediction. We did not get to swim or fish. We did a lot of flying off an unimproved airstrip.

It was shortly after we returned from bivouac that we left Alliance for Fort Wayne, Indiana.

August 23, 1943

Dear Folks,

We've been busy up here as usual. Not too much flying time, but lots of time spent sitting out under the plane waiting for directions, etc.

Alliance Army Air Base had its dedication yesterday. Fifty-nine thousand people came to see the show. It must've been pretty good, because there were some good items on the program.

We put on a mock invasion of the air base, and the 73d brought in the gliders.

I had my instrument check a few days ago and made it OK, so now I can take off in ceiling zero but doubt if I ever will, unless there's no other way out.

I think we're going on a bivouac sometime this week. The site will be around Hot Springs, South Dakota, somewhere, so we'll all be able to catch up on our fishing, swimming, and sleeping under pine trees. Also, we'll catch up on working off a makeshift airport.

We are now known as the "Fighting 73d—Paratrooper Eradicators Deluxe." About six of our pilots (I wasn't on hand) made twice that many "peashooter" officers say "uncle" in a sort of a free-for-all that started from just a little flare-up. The peashooters, following their usual tactics, happened on one of our guys. He was holding his own pretty well, although out-

Airborne troops pass in review at the Dedication Day parade, Alliance Army Air Base, August, 1943. Photo courtesy the Knight Museum, Alliance, Nebraska

Display of CG-4A gliders on Dedication Day at Alliance Army Air Base. Photo courtesy the Knight Museum Alliance, Nebraska

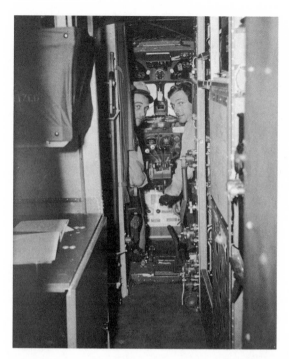

View of a C-47 cockpit, looking forward from the navigator's and radio operator's stations. Photo courtesy of the Knight Museum, Alliance, Nebraska

C-47s "buzz" the field on Dedication Day at Alliance Army Air Base. Photo courtesy the Knight Museum, Alliance, Nebraska

numbered twelve to one, but when he summoned five other guys to help him, it was just a massacre—paratroopers all over the floor. It wasn't a very important event, and not very gentlemanly, but it exploded the myth that peashooters are supermen, and now they don't act so darned arrogant. The 73d is now the toast of the 434th Group.

I can't think of any more news—you can see by that last item that I've been digging pretty deep.

Am going to try to write two letters tonight, but I doubt if I'll make it. Sure am getting sleepy.

Write soon.

Love to all,
Billy

IT ALL COMES DOWN TO FLYING A NICE, TIGHT FORMATION

Nothing was more important to the troop-carrier pilot than the ability to fly wingtip to wingtip with other pilots in his squadron. There was good reason for this. We were not dropping bombs. We were dropping soldiers (or delivering them in gliders), and it was important that these airborne fighters hit the ground together—as squads, platoons, battalions, whatever—so they could take coordinated action immediately. The term for the desired result on the drop zone was "unit integrity."

You could not achieve unit integrity if your aircraft were flown in a loose formation or if individual aircraft were out of position. It was a rule of thumb that the best squadron was the one that flew the tightest formation. If the formation was ragged, you had work to do.

As cadets we had been introduced to formation flying. We had learned to overcome the natural desire to maintain a safe distance from other aircraft and, instead, to snuggle up. It required a degree of hand-eye coordination and intense concentration. It was hard work but it looked good. In fact, it was the accepted way to show off.

As a cadet, I had last flown formation in the AT-6 advanced trainer, an ideal airplane for the job. The lumbering C-47, I assumed, would be the worst formation airplane imaginable. I was happily surprised to find the ungainly looking transport was almost as responsive to controls as the AT-6 had been. Only in terms of power was the C-47's responsiveness lacking. If you allowed the plane to lag out of position, you would be slow to catch up. But we learned to deal with that drawback.

During our time at Alliance, air corps and airborne planners were still firming up formation procedures. How best could some fifty airplanes converge over a single drop zone or (in the case of gliders) landing zone without running into each other? Would the most effective pattern be the standard V (a leader and two wingmen), a V of Vs (essentially, a nine-ship V), or an echelon (multiple wingmen attached to one leader)?

In the process of developing and mastering the most efficient formation patterns, the 73d suffered a major accident.

The following excerpt is from the front page of the *Alliance Times-Herald,* July 13, 1943:

> *Eight Killed as Planes Crash near Hemingford*
> Eight men from the Alliance Army Air Base, including four officers and four non-commissioned officers, were instantly killed at 4:30 Saturday afternoon when two large C-47 transport planes on a routine group formation training flight collided in midair and crashed to the ground on the Louis Bowers ranch, 25 miles west of Hemingford on Highway 87.

I did not write home about this. It made no sense to broadcast bad news. But formation flying came up a lot in my letters around this time because that is what we were doing. And it was an exhilarating thing to do when conditions were right. That meant having smooth air, an important audience, empty planes, and a responsible position in the formation for my airplane, my favorite being the lead plane in the second or third V of Vs. In that position, a pilot who understood the nuances of good formation flying could make things easier for at least eight other pilots, and he could very positively affect the looks of the whole formation.

If we flew empty airplanes, that meant we were doing the formation just for show. We were then only simulating what we would do in a real delivery of paratroopers. It was no coincidence that our best formations were the simulated ones when our airplanes were empty. We could come over the reviewing stand at an absurdly low altitude and at a comfortably fast airspeed. Some forty airplanes arriving that way sounded like a Hell's Angels convention rolling into town.

With paratroopers on board it was difficult to maintain tight formation over a DZ (drop zone). Airspeed had to be reduced to a maximum of 120 mph to minimize the windblast that the trooper jumped into. The airplane's center of gravity went a little crazy as troopers jumped and the load shifted. Flight controls turned mushy because of the slow speed. You were flirting with a power-on stall. It was easy to fall into the propwash (turbulence) stirred up by the airplanes ahead.

A daytime live drop was hard work. A nighttime live drop was harder still.

Towing gliders in formation was not as difficult as it would seem. As I recall, we towed them in two-ship elements, which appeared as a long, slow train of tow ships and gliders.

The CG-4A glider could carry men or a jeep or a small artillery piece, even a baby bulldozer. Fully loaded, it grossed more than seven thousand pounds. On takeoff, the glider cleared the ground first, then the tow ship. It was all the C-47 could do to maintain 110 mph with a loaded glider at the end of the nylon towrope. Throttles remained at full-forward takeoff setting, or close to it, for the duration of the flight. The airplane would shudder along, nose-high, hanging on the props.

THE FACTORY DECLARES ME
A FINISHED PRODUCT

The pilot factory was not through with me when I graduated and got my wings. I knew that now. It took nine more months of training in an operational setting (most of it at Alliance) in order to prepare me to fly an airplane to a combat theater and perform the missions that would be required of me.

As a troop-carrier pilot, I considered myself a mixed breed of aviator—part flyboy to be sure, but part truck driver, too, and part dogface GI. I just did not fit the picture that the Wild Blue Yonder brought to mind.

The fighter jocks fit the picture. So did the pilots of the B-17s and the B-24s and the lesser bombers. They were coming to grips with the enemy at the controls of real warplanes.

The crate we flew was as goofy and as harmless as it looked.

Our C-47s looked especially bad because we often flew them with the cargo doors removed. The door was where the paratroopers jumped out. The door was easy to remove, but you still had to contend with the door hinges that stuck out from the door frame into the door opening. As a jumping trooper could get snagged on a hinge, the hinges were carefully bandaged with layers of duct tape, which took a lot of time.

After a jump, it did not make sense to remove all that carefully applied tape and rehang the door. You would probably be dropping troops again that day or the next, or the next week.

And so it came to pass that a gaping cavity in the side of the fuselage (from which might flutter loose ends of duct tape) became an identifying mark of a troop-carrier C-47.

Another aspect of our uniqueness was our contingent of glider pilots. No other arm of the air corps had glider pilots. These young men had come into the glider program by many different avenues. Some had been light-plane pilots. Others were attracted to the program because it promised opportunity for independent, daredevil action. All seemed adjusted to the uncertainty and hazards associated with their mission.

As a group, though, the glider pilots had the disadvantage of not having enough to do. In training, as it would prove to be in a combat theater, as well, they could be terribly busy for a short time and then dormant for months. It was not their fault; it was a reflection of the glider's role in the big picture. The glider was not a tool to be used every day. It was designed for the big deals, and those did not come along very often.

The glider pilots did what they could to make themselves useful when the gliders were not flying. Some took over major squadron administrative duties. Others logged copilot time on the C-47s when regular "power pilots" were in short supply.

In September, 1943, the flight crews of the 73d Squadron (together with those of the rest of the 434th Group) departed Alliance for Baer Field in Fort Wayne, Indiana, to be outfitted for a flight to England and an indefinite assignment to the European theater of operations. Big auxiliary fuel tanks were installed in the cabins of our C-47s. These so-called cabin tanks would give us the range we needed to fly the Northern Route to Europe. The logistical minutiae required for the trip was completed within a few weeks.

We took off at 7:00 one morning in late September. Some of us had partied until the wee hours. A few of us had never gone to sleep. You could usually get away with that in a C-47. It was not an airplane that liked to turn around and bite you.

If I wrote home from Fort Wayne, the letters did not survive. Telephoning would have been relatively easy. That is probably how I kept in touch and finally said goodbye.

TO WAR BY THE NORTHERN ROUTE

I was part of a five-man crew. The copilot was Clayton Gardner, a good-looking young Down-Easter from Millinocket, Maine, who would later graduate to first pilot and a crew of his own. The navigator was Jim Taylor, from Minneapolis—smart, dependable, and old enough (mid- or late twenties probably) to exude authority. The crew chief (or aerial engineer) was George O'Sullivan, a Bostonian probably in his late thirties, who had a delightful personality and accent and was rumored to have attended Harvard. The radio operator was Herschel Lyons who was, I believe, from a town in western Missouri.

Our itinerary was Fort Wayne to Presque Isle, Maine; then to Goose Bay, Labrador; then to Greenland; then to Iceland; then to Prestwick, Scotland; then to our new base in England, which turned out to be near Nottingham. The trip proved to be exciting, sometimes wildly so.

Fort Wayne to Presque Isle

Our course took us directly over Niagara Falls. I could not resist circling the falls a time or two. As we circled we used the fuel selector to switch from wing tanks to the cabin tank, and both engines abruptly quit. I do not recall just what we had done wrong, but Gardner or O'Sullivan quickly solved the problem, and we got the engines restarted and continued on our way. Somewhere over Maine we spotted a moose in a pretty little lake deep in the woods.

We were at Presque Isle for one day at most. All I remember is that there was heavy traffic of air crews flying to and from England on the Northern Route of the air transport command. Ferry pilots were returning from England to pick up more planes for delivery. Heading east with my group was a large group of B-25s in desert colors, destined for North Africa or Sicily, I suppose.

Presque Isle to Goose Bay

All transient crews were briefed together for the flight to Labrador. There was the usual report on weather conditions, current and predicted. Then the main briefing officer really got my attention. You will be flying over the Gulf of the St. Lawrence, he said, so keep your eyes peeled for German subs and report any you see. I did not see any subs, but it was not because I was not looking.

Of the day or two or three we spent at Goose Bay, all I remember is a fishing trip. The picture is very hazy. We were on a river. We had a guide and two rowboats. The water was swift and cold. The boats did not have enough freeboard to suit me, but we did not swamp. And we did not catch any fish either.

Goose Bay to Greenland

Somebody decided we would fly to Greenland in formation. We took off, formed up, and headed east. About ten minutes after takeoff we ran into heavy snow. The formation leader radioed to us that, on his signal, we were to follow the formation-dispersal procedure that we had been practicing for several months. It worked. A safe separation was established between airplanes, and we continued on our way to Greenland in the snow.

Some time later we came out of the snow into a clear blue sky, and, dead ahead, there was Greenland. It was probably seventy-five or a hundred miles away, but the visibility was so crystal-clear, it looked very close. Everything sparkled in that scene—the sky, the water, and the glittering shape of Greenland.

The air base had the strange name of Bluie West 1. It lay at the end of a fjord and had a single runway that ran a little uphill in the landing direction and downhill on takeoff. When you committed to land, you could not change your mind.

We were all able to spend a few days in Greenland. You could walk outside the base and be in a pristine wilderness of sheer cliffs and glacier-fed streams. We spent the first full day that we were there exploring. We hiked and climbed together for a few hours, then we decided to split up and regroup at an appointed time. It was late in the day when we assembled to hike back to the base. Everybody showed up except Hugh Gunn.

Hugh was a strapping young man who had come straight to flight school from a cattle ranch in Wyoming. Hugh could take care of himself better than any of the rest of us. But we feared he could have fallen and broken a leg, or worse. The temperature would drop below freezing pretty soon. We fired our .45s and yelled until twilight. Then somebody remembered that there was a rescue team at the base with dogs, sleds, and paramedical gear.

The rescue guys refused to start a search at night, so we went to the barracks, got our flashlights, and hiked back out to where we had been that afternoon, yelling and shooting and listening for a response from Hugh. The northern lights were spectacular that night. Normally, it would have been a thrilling experience, but we were gloomy when we gave up the search and headed back to the base, worried that Hugh, if he were still alive, would not survive the night.

We found Hugh on his bunk in the barracks, more than a little tipsy, and eager to tell us about the British officers from a corvette in the harbor who had been out hiking, too, and who had invited Hugh to join them for dinner and drinks aboard their vessel.

We pulled Hugh out of his bunk, dumped him on the floor, and went to the mess hall to get ourselves hot coffee and something to eat.

It probably was the next day when O'Sullivan, the crew chief, told me that we needed a new magneto on one engine and that it would have to be shipped from the States. So my crew and I had to watch everybody else take off for Iceland. The replacement magneto did not arrive for a week or two. In the PX, I found a copy of *Men at War*, the favorite war stories of Ernest Hemmingway, collected and edited by the author. The book helped relieve the frustration caused by the wait.

Greenland to Iceland

We flew over the Greenland Ice Cap, a veritable mountain of ice that rises as high as twelve thousand feet. We must have skirted the peak, because with the load we were carrying, it would have been a struggle to reach twelve thousand feet.

It was snowing when we landed in Iceland. It was snowing when we left. Maybe that is why I remember the base as being underground, everything but the runways. I am sure that was not true.

Iceland to Scotland

We were in Iceland just long enough to eat dinner, sleep a few hours, eat breakfast, and get briefed for the next leg of the trip. I believe we were told that we were the last twin-engine airplane to be cleared for the

Northern Route that year. Sure enough, all the other pilots in the briefing seemed to be flying B-17s. Andy Devine (the comedian) asked if he could fly with us to England, where he was to join a USO group. I had to tell him we were already overloaded.

After takeoff we broke out of the snow and into the clear at about six thousand feet. At the same time, a B-17 appeared just off my left wing-tip in the same climb attitude as my airplane. It was a chilling sight, the closest I had ever come to another airplane in flight, unintentionally. Somebody had goofed.

Soon we were back in snow and ice, and some of the ice was sticking. I tried to get above the ice but could not. The glaze we had already picked up was proving a burden, and the prospect of collecting more was a real concern. I decided to descend, hoping to find air warm enough to thaw the ice we had collected and prevent further icing. The ceiling was low—maybe three hundred to four hundred feet—and that is where we finally found an air temperature above freezing. We were flying so low at times that it was hard to distinguish between ice sloughing off the airplane and spume flying off the tops of the huge waves just below.

Those waves were generated by the gale into which we were flying directly. It had already slowed us to the point that we could not possibly reach our destination of Prestwick, Scotland.

The Isle of Lewis is the outermost of the Hebrides, and it was the first land we had seen since Greenland (Iceland having been invisible to us due to snow). The RAF maintained an airstrip at the northern tip of the island, and that is where we landed.

The closest town was Stornoway. We must have been among the very few Americans who had been there up to that time. Everybody we saw was apple-cheeked—from the wind, we supposed, because it never stopped blowing. The tweed in the jackets the men wore looked about an inch thick.

Scotland to Fulbeck, England

The flight from Stornoway to Prestwick, Scotland, was short and un-eventful. At Prestwick an RAF navigator was assigned to our crew. We thought this unnecessary since we already had a navigator who had just navigated us across the Atlantic. We thought differently once we were airborne over northern England. What we saw below was a totally unfamiliar landscape. There were no right angles, no grids of roads and fencerows. The countryside extended as far as we could see in a puzzling pattern that resembled an irregular paisley design. We would get used to it, but that first day over England we would have never found our way to Fulbeck without the help of the RAF.

As we arrived over the airfield, just before we entered the traffic pattern, one engine quit. We made a routine engine-out landing, all of us thankful that the engine had not quit a few days before when we had been icing up over the North Atlantic.

IMPRESSIONS OF ENGLAND

October, 1943, to April, 1944

At Fulbeck, an airfield near Nottingham, the 73d and the other squadrons of the 434th Troop Carrier Group assembled and took stock of our new surroundings. It was obvious that our food service was in the hands (temporarily) of the RAF. One clue was that dessert was always butterscotch pudding. The other clue was that the arm that plunged the scoop into the garbage-can-sized container to bring out the pudding wore a sleeve of RAF blue, crusted with flecks of butterscotch.

I could put up with the pudding. I was an Anglophile to begin with. On top of that, I was sensitive to the privations that the British had suffered. I could also put up with the honey buckets in the latrines, the cold-water showers, and the tiny coal-burning stoves (we called them cigarette lighters) that were supposed to heat our Quonset huts and did not.

Just being in England fascinated me. We had to move our base of operations three times during our first three months, from Fulbeck to Welford Park, and then to Aldermaston, west of Reading. I am sure the moves were logistical hassles. But they offered us new things to see, and I took it all in.

Most of my letters now were V-mails. They are short and they do not say much about our flying training because of military censorship. One episode I did not write home about had nothing to do with flying.

A Long Night in Nottingham

The motor pool had set up a shuttle service between the air base and the city of Nottingham. It was to be the first English city any of us would see. And talk about luck—it was the one English city (outside London) that we already had a romantic attachment to, thanks to Robin Hood. We all hopped on the shuttle truck at the first opportunity.

Nottingham had a large dance hall downtown. It did not take us long to find it and to get out on the floor. I paired off with a girl who did not seem to mind my footwork, and we stayed together until the band packed up. I asked an MP when the next shuttle left for the air base, and he told me that the last shuttle had already left.

While I was trying to think about what to do next, the girl told me that I could stay at her house. It was a long walk. She lived (with her mother and father, it turned out) in a respectable-looking rowhouse, comparable to what you might see in an older American city. We sat on a couch in the parlor for a short time, then the girl excused herself and left through French doors that opened on a dining room. I had the impression she was coming back to the parlor, but she did not.

I eventually stood up, did some jumping jacks to warm myself against the chill of the dark room, and decided to get out of there. But all the doors were locked. The parlor had become a prison. I could not even settle myself down with a cigarette, because I had run out of matches during the walk to the house. I did not want to raise a ruckus and wake up the whole family. I was, after all, a guest. Besides, I was curious to see how the whole thing would play out. Hours passed. It was still dark when I heard the first noises. They sounded like kitchen noises. The mother, I figured, was fixing breakfast. Then two muffled voices were talking, in the kitchen, presumably. Mother and father, I guessed. They obviously did not know that a stranger from a faraway country was sitting in their parlor, starving for a cigarette. Finally, a third voice, the girl. There was a brief conversation, then the French doors opened and the girl, in a bathrobe, invited me up a short flight of stairs to the kitchen where I joined the family for breakfast before taking my leave and walking back to catch the shuttle.

My hut mates in the Quonset hut at the air base wanted to know how I had spent the night. I did not tell them the whole truth.

What follows are some excerpts from letters written while I was at Fulbeck and Welford Park.

About barracks life:
> (Dec. 30) We didn't do much on Christmas Day, but everything was nice and quiet. I'll mention a few things that would come in handy in case you can send them. The first is hair oil, Vaseline preferred; Schick injector razor blades; some stationery;

and any amount of that fudge and divinity you mentioned. We get all the cigarettes we need.

(Jan. 8) Our latest delicacy over at the mess hall is toast—Limey bread toasted on forks over one of the little stoves in the room. It really tastes good for some reason. We spend hours eating and toasting.

(Jan. 13) When I come home I'm going to give you all about a week's warning, so there'll be plenty of hot water. Just bathed and shaved in ice water.

(Jan. 19) We had rice pudding with raisins last night and I thought how much it lacked in comparison with yours, Mom. It didn't taste bad, though. It's been a little better than four months since we pulled out of Baer Field and I can't make up my mind whether the time has passed quickly or just dragged. It does seem like years since I've seen the States.

(Jan. 19) You should see me now, Nancy. You would enjoy it very much. I sweep and wash clothes and dust and do all of those things I used to sit back and watch you do. I really have a lot of trouble writing to you, Nancy—not because I don't want to, but because I can't decide what you want me to talk about. You're past the paper-doll age, and you're still quite a few years from college, so that puts you right at the time of a girl's life when she wants to be a social worker or a newshound or just any kind of a career girl. Maybe I'm all wrong.

(Feb. 7) I have an egg in my dresser drawer that a friend brought me the other day. [A real egg was precious over there.] Think I'll save it for my birthday. Just finished about the best book I ever read—*A Tree Grows in Brooklyn*. It was so good that toward the end I read only five pages at a time to postpone the ending as long as possible.

(Feb. 13) We were all sewing yesterday. Everybody in the hut had a needle and thread and was working on something. The results were disastrous for the clothing. One fellow sewed his shirt to a raincoat, another sewed the sleeve of his blouse together. Trying to remodel a hat, I failed completely. The hat is all apart now and some important section of it is lost.

About keeping warm:

(Jan. 13) Our biggest problem is keeping warm and clean. Fuel (coal) is very scarce, and last night we chopped up a dresser and burned it to get the dampness out of the hut. Hot water also is at a premium and we are masters of the art of cold-water bathing and shaving.

(Jan. 21) I was out in a field by the hut yesterday chopping away at a royal rail fence, and I flushed a covey of partridges. They sounded and looked just like quail but were a lot bigger.

(Jan. 28) The other day we took a truck out to a little village and persuaded a farmer to let us hack up a few of his less choice pieces of timber for our fire. We chopped for about an hour and filled the truck. The wood has lasted for a week and we still have some left.

About weather:

(Jan. 13) The weather here is not something I'm supposed to talk about, but I can tell you that all the birds have instrument ratings.

(Jan. 25) You should hear the wind howl tonight—just as bad as Alliance, and it's been blowing that way for three days now. I guess it's averaging about thirty-five miles per hour. Went up this afternoon for just a little formation practice and it was really rough. The wings were flapping like birds' wings.

About Smitty:

(Jan. 13) Smitty and I flew this afternoon. It was a bad day, and we had the air to ourselves, so we practiced a few crosswind landings, buzzed around the countryside looking at castles, etc. Smitty cut an engine on me on the first takeoff, and I thought it was the real thing. I really sweated before I got it feathered and got a little altitude.

(Jan. 16) We had a bunch of weather sneak in here this afternoon and it caught a lot of the guys up in the air. We were sweating Smitty out but just heard that he landed safely at another base. [It was one of some fifteen RAF bases equipped with a system called FIDO. That was the acronym for Fog Investigation Dispersal Operation. FIDO literally burned out a tunnel in the fog for the length of the runway. It consisted of gasoline pipes running the length of the runway on both sides. The gasoline was vaporized then forced into perforated pipes and lighted. Heat produced by the flames lifted the fog, creating the fog-free tunnel. Using FIDO was like landing between two walls of flame. It was a last resort. Only the most skilled pilots possessed the confidence and steadiness required. Pilots died trying to land by means of FIDO the very afternoon that Smitty succeeded. The RAF insisted that he stay with them an extra day so they could properly wine and dine him.]

(March 22) Smitty just came in for a few words and pulled out again. He is quite a guy and really a hot pilot. He's one of those natural born one-in-a-thousand fliers. He'd probably shine in any plane.

(May 24) Smitty is a flight leader now, and as I've told you before, I guess, the best pilot in the group in my estimation. What Smitty doesn't know about flying just isn't worth knowing.

About the scene:

(Jan. 2) We saw a foxhunt from the air the other day. It was right close to the field. A bunch of Joes were running around in circles with red coats and white horses trying to corner the fox. It was a pretty sight.

(Jan. 22) Nancy, you should've been with me yesterday afternoon. I went into town and attended a tea dance. They had a little three-piece band that stuck to waltzes all afternoon. Big signs on the wall emphasized that there would be no jitterbugging in this dance hall, and tea and crumpets in the corner. It was all so quiet and staid that Jack (Miser) and I just stood there looking over each other's shoulder for about an hour and finally left. There was a big dance that night in honor of a bunch of Polish fliers, and it was more our style. At least we could talk above a whisper without being conspicuous.

(March 28) Dear Sis, I'm listening to our coveted American Forces program straight from the States—our only source of jive and up-to-date music. Boy, it's good. I have a few favorite pieces that they play pretty often, "Close to You" is one, and I'm beginning to like "Shoo, Shoo, Baby." There's a big musical that's been running for a long time in London called *The Lisbon Story*. It's really good, especially a song about Pedro the Fisherman, which he whistles partway through. I've been wondering if it's hit the States. We hear a lot of Sinatra records where the audience screams so loud that Frankie is almost extinguished. Also hear about "Moonlight Sinatra Clubs" and "Girls-Who-Would-Lay-Down-Their-Lives-and-Die-for-Frank-Sinatra Clubs." You aren't a member, are you?

(April 2) We get to stay out overnight about twice a month and that's about all that we can afford because everything is so darned expensive. They have the pound note over here that looks like our dollar and is the thing they base their currency on. A pound is equal to four of our dollars, but we never think of that and throw them away just like they were bucks, and usually we blow everything on one pass and sit around broke for the rest of the month.

(April 8) Today is Easter. Just had fried chicken up at the mess hall. I'm waiting around to fly later on this afternoon. It's pretty dreary out today. Yesterday would've been the ideal Easter—warm, sunny, and all kinds of flowers blooming. Every house around here has a big flower garden and most people have their own glass hothouses just for flower growing.

About recreation:

(Feb. 10) They finally gave us a good break—everybody was getting pretty tired. We got a plane and had a regular old cross-country like we used to take every weekend up in Alliance. Jack, several other guys, and I took one over to a resort town on the coast (Blackpool). It's quite a place in peacetime and was still lively enough to be a lot of fun. I ice-skated, dug clams, and did all kinds of things that we don't have an opportunity to do very often. It was a swell trip, and even though I was more fatigued on returning than I was before I started, it was refreshing.

Just about the time I got back from that jaunt, I had a forty-eight-hour pass come through, so Smitty and I took off for the big town (London). We took it easy—bought a few socks and some handkerchiefs, saw a show, and just generally took it easy. Saw an old 42-J man in London. We had a short bull session, and I promised to drop over and see him sometime.

About the war:

(Feb. 7) I am listening to the radio—some German station, and the commentator is really talking hard, probably trying to finish up before the B-17s come over. We hear Lord Haw Haw occasionally, and he's very funny. It's fantastic the way he can change German defeats into victories, or at least strategic withdrawals. He doesn't sound very convincing though.

(Feb. 12) Dad, I'm sitting down here in the Squadron Intelligence Department, and up on the wall they have a big map of the Russian Front showing all the wedges and salients, etc. Right now the Russians have another hundred thousand Germans trapped, and I've been thinking of the day way back a couple of Julys ago when you said they could and no one else seemed to think so.

(Feb. 20) Daddy, you would really enjoy listening to these propaganda programs put out by the Jerries. They analyze the news in English and they manage somehow to analyze everything in their favor. They had a terrible time analyzing a hundred thousand men out of that trap in the Ukraine, but tonight they called Stalin a liar and said that the trapped men had made contact with the rescuers and everything was OK.

A 48-HOUR PASS USUALLY MEANS ANOTHER TRIP TO LONDON

My letters mention London only briefly. One describes stately Grosvenor House: "The place consists of a gigantic Officers' Mess with really good food and reading and writing rooms, etc. The whole place is very extravagant-looking as it was one of London's classic hotels before it was taken over by the army."

Of course, I did not go to London at least twenty times just to eat dinner at Grosvenor House. What drew me (and, I suspect, most of us) to foggy, blacked-out, bombed-out London were the exciting and naughty aspects of the city. I never did see Big Ben or the British Museum. London was my favorite destination because it seemed the likeliest place to find female companionship, for which we were starved. The city did not beat around the bush in promoting sex. The male sidewalk hucksters who sold flashlights with the cry, "Torches, torches, get your torches here!" also sold condoms. When someone in uniform walked by, the salesman would lower his "Torches!" shout to a discreet stage whisper, and the message would change to "Condoms, condoms, condoms." Picadilly commandos (London's streetwalkers) were everywhere.

The best places to find a date were the little private bars that catered to Americans, especially American air crews. These bars served a niche market. The proprietor or proprietress needed just enough space for a bar and a few tables. The clubs were named for their target customers: The American Club, or The Pilots' Lounge, for example. Membership cards were printed (but rarely needed to be shown). Apparently, word got around to neighborhood women that the club was a good place to meet a guy. The object did not have to be sex, and it probably was not, as far as the women were concerned. British conventions at the time made it difficult for a nice girl to meet a male stranger. The clubs met a need.

Most young British women wore a uniform of some kind. They were in the auxiliary services of the army, navy, or RAF, or in the land army where they worked in the fields, taking the place of farmers who had gone off to fight. There were also young women from the Continent whose countries had been overrun by the Nazis. I met a girl from Budapest who had fled to London with her parents. They lived in an upscale apartment hotel. She showed me a snapshot of herself standing between two big brothers who looked like twins and who held huge, scimitar-like swords. If the photo was meant to be a warning, the message got through to me.

The most significant influences on life in London during the time of my visits were the Nazi V-weapons: the V-1 missile, or "buzz-bomb," and the V-2 rocket, a ballistic missile that was the forerunner of today's intercontinental missiles. More than nine thousand of these weapons were fired at Britain (primarily London) between June of 1944 and March of 1945. Each weapon delivered a warhead that contained two thousand pounds of high explosives.

The V-1s were to me the more disturbing of the two missiles because they could be heard as they approached. In the silence that followed the warning siren, the putt-putt of the V-1's ramjet engine would become discernable and then increasingly distinct as the weapon drew closer. Then the putt-putts would stop. The few seconds of silence that followed meant the missile was plunging into the city. The explosion told you where.

I did most of my listening to the putt-putts (and to the totally unannounced explosions of the V-2 rockets) in a guest room at the Berners Hotel in the West End of London. I do not remember how I discovered the Berners but it was a primary reason I went back to London again and again. The hotel had been built in 1835, and I imagined that the country gentry would have liked to stay there when they came to London to shop. The bathtub was huge, as were all the bathroom fixtures and the bed. The Berners was a solidly satisfying hotel then, and, with a four-star rating and an attractively illustrated Web site, it apparently still is.

London might not have been so alluring had I been awake to what was close at hand. A beautiful stretch of the Thames River ran just a few miles past the base at Aldermaston. There were rental canoes as well as punts. Landscaped lawns ran down to the water's edge. Tea shops were located at convenient intervals to serve boaters. The lock operator four or five miles upstream would accommodate an individual canoe if you wanted to paddle farther toward the headwaters. All this I did not know at the time. Boris Shvetzoff told me all about it a few years ago. Boris had been a sergeant in the 73d Squadron Tech Supply. He was also an experienced canoeist and was quick to discover the upper Thames. That is where he spent his off-duty time. That is where I would spend mine if I had it to do over again.

A NEW CO TAKES OVER AND THE GROUP SHAPES UP

My squadron, the 73d, was one of four in the 434th Group. We always had the other squadrons to measure ourselves against. If we compared satisfactorily, there was nothing major to worry about. That was the prevailing attitude.

It did not occur to us that our whole quartet of squadrons might have allowed sloppiness to creep in on a wholesale basis. But that is what happened, and it had a bad effect on the way we flew, the food we ate, the maintenance of our airplanes, and our general appearance as a military organization.

Then one day it must have dawned on everybody who was in the air at that time that we were a dysfunctional group. On that day, as I recall, the ceiling was about six hundred feet and visibility was less than a mile. We were trying to form up in a forty-odd–ship formation behind our group commander, and the low clouds and restricted visibility were making it difficult. "You're just a bunch of schoolboys!" the colonel shouted into our headphones. "You fly like a bunch of schoolboys!"

As it turned out, the "schoolboy" was the formation leader, our commanding officer. He was sacked a few weeks later. We got a new CO, a fifty-one-year-old former airline captain and executive whose name was William Whitacre. Later the army newspaper *Stars & Stripes* would refer to the 434th Group as "Whitacre's Wonders," and we would fly a demonstration formation for Winston Churchill.

Three years later, in 1946, when I was back in college on the GI Bill, my English teacher asked the class to write an expository piece about a person who had been influential in our life, I titled my piece "New CO." Here it is:

The majority of the great men of World War II were known only to the men who served with them or under them. I had the privilege of serving under one of these men who, although he would not qualify as a hero according to accepted standards, was idolized by the unit that he commanded.

Colonel Whitacre took over command of our group with the knowledge that three previous commanders had tried to weld the outfit into some semblance of an organized, disciplined unit, had failed, and had each been relieved of his command. He was taking a group that had become extremely prejudiced against group commanders. A group that now waited impatiently — curious to see how best it would wreck the plans of this latest arrival to that unpopular position.

The colonel moved in one morning and announced that he would speak to the entire unit that afternoon. That was something we had not expected, since all of Colonel Whitacre's predecessors had chosen to run the group by means of customary channels and seldom were seen outside of headquarters. The idea that this new colonel wanted to address everyone in person was something unusual, and it intrigued even the most chronic adherents to the group policy of avoidance of duty.

That afternoon the base theater bulged with the first mass meeting of the unit since its activation. There was a quick surge of whispers followed by tense silence as the rear door opened and Colonel Whitacre walked in and down the center aisle to the stage. We looked and saw him, small and erect, moving up the steps alone. There was no trail of staff officers behind him, nobody to introduce him. He turned, faced the room, and put one hand in his pocket while the audience sized him up.

He was beyond middle age, near fifty, I guessed, but his bearing was of West Point caliber. His stance was natural, not stiff, and the set of his shoulders was confident rather than pompous. He moved his head slowly as his gaze swept the big room, and the light showed sparse gray hair, especially thin down the middle. His eyes dominated the other features. They seemed to be blue or gray, very keen, with fine little crow's-feet at the corners, and deeper, more serious wrinkles underneath. There was nothing cold or impersonal about his eyes. They alone would have been enough to preserve the absolute silence that filled the room.

He spoke quietly, and in spite of the gentleness of tone there was a solid punch behind each word. We would work hard beginning that afternoon. We would fly so many hours a month. The mess halls would be cleaned up. The only mention he made of our past conduct regarded discipline. He said it was very lax and that we would correct that by rising at 5:30 every morning and drilling for one hour before breakfast. He used profanity only once, to emphasize one of his special desires: "And the goddamned bar will close at midnight!" He finished and everyone rose and faced straight ahead in the first display of military courtesy seen in a long time while the new commander walked back down the aisle to the rear door.

The professor called my piece "a good, clean portrait" but graded it an "S-minus," which would have corresponded to a B-minus. I felt I had let Colonel Whitacre down.

FINAL RUN-UP TO D-DAY

March to June, 1944

The winter of 1943–44 was probably a typical English winter, gray and wet. We found it unexpectedly dark, beyond anything we had experienced. Our medics became concerned that the absence of sunshine was affecting our health.

This resulted in the setting up of a tanning salon on the base. A schedule was determined that allowed each of us time under the sun lamp. We had to wear large round, protective goggles. These sessions produced a tan of varying darkness or redness except on the skin around the eyes that was covered by the goggles. It remained as pallid as before. The effect was that of a mask, similar to the mask on the face of a raccoon, except with the shades of dark and light reversed. As soon as we got a good look at ourselves and each other, the tanning salon was shut down.

As winter turned into spring, we moved from our dreary base north of London to a more attractive airfield west of London, near Reading. The English gardens were beginning to bloom and my apparent good spirits are reflected in the following excerpts from happy V-mails written just prior to D-Day.

About our new base at Aldermaston:
    (March 5) Tonight I'm writing from a sharp little room that Jack (Miser) and I call home now. We moved, and our new quarters are really super. Jack and I have a private room, two beds, two big lockers, a dresser, washbasin, and a big wood stove. It's the best thing we've had in the way of quarters since Baer Field.

The author in the spring of 1944 at Aldermaston Air Base, England.

(March 28) This field is really swell [for the hundredth time]. There is a little hamlet sort of mingled in with the barracks, etc., and a lady about a block from here does my laundry and I get it in about five days. There is a grocery also, but we don't have any coupons, so the only thing we can buy is mousetraps. The mice have left us, by the way. We really left them, I guess. Don't think I told you about all the compliments received on your candy. There were too many, in fact, and now the guys watch for my packages as much as they do for their own.

About putting on a show for Churchill:

(March 25) I think that it will be OK to tell you about a demonstration we made the other day. Our audience consisted of Churchill and the whole invasion staff. It was a good demonstration, and I think that they were all impressed—at least that's what the Old Man said. I'm going to be pretty busy this afternoon, and it's almost afternoon right now, so I'd better go get into harness. We just had our regular Saturday inspection and the place really shines.

Flight time near 1,000 hours:

(March 28) Dear Dad, thought I would hit a thousand hours by the end of this month, but they've called off a few flights and I don't think I can make it in three days. Only lack twelve hours now.

One of the first things I would like to do when I get back and everything settles down is to buy a good plane and keep it out at Broyton's or someplace and give you some lessons. We could make a weekend fishing trip to the Caney Fork or Lake Okeechobee in less time than it would take to go to the Gasconade [river in the Missouri Ozark foothills] by Buick.

Really is soft this afternoon, nothing to do but lie in the sack. Think I'll try to get a bicycle and tour around the countryside a little later. We're flying tonight, so the relaxing we do in the evening will have to be this afternoon.

The scene:

(May 3) I'm flying tonight so will write my daily letter this afternoon. This will make three days in succession that I haven't failed.

You should see the air traffic around this island. There is always a plane somewhere overhead, and you can scan the skies any time and pick out formations of them. This is a wonderful place to develop a good eye for aircraft identification.

Nancy, you and I must look a lot alike because everybody says so whenever they see your picture. Mom says you're going to get all dolled up again and have some more made. Send them over here for sure if you do.

Daddy, I would've never believed it a few years ago, but there is really some beautiful country around here—really wild and uninhabited. We've had opportunities lately to fly over unsettled parts of Wales and Scotland, and there are pinewoods and mountain streams that almost compare with Colorado's.

Most of the fishing streams around here are small little creeks with carefully trimmed and packed banks. You would never imagine that a fish would be so cultivated as to live in such artificial-looking surroundings, but there are some big ones, all right.

Every hole has a fish in it that's sort of a legend, and all the local anglers patiently match wits with him for their—the angler's—whole life. The fish never seems to die. Some inns have tremendous speckled and brook trout mounted on plaques with bronze plates inscribed with the name of the fish, the angler who made the grade, and the date of the catch, some of them dating back to the mid-1800s. Still, they don't fish right over here, even if it *is* where Izaac Walton started the whole thing.

Seems like we have a training film to attend, so, so long for now.

"Spike" the dog:

(May 6) I don't know what kind of dog to settle on—a pointer or setter would be swell, anything along that line. What would you think of a wirehair terrier?

I had a little mongrel around here for a few days. We called him "Spike," and all he wanted to do was eat and sleep. Every night someone would come in and put Spike in the sack with me and I'd wake up in the morning with his face about six inches from mine. He finally got all the eating and sleeping he wanted and went off again looking for greener pastures.

Have to eat dinner now and go to work.

Recreation:

(June 1) I went swimming again since I last wrote you, and the water was quite a bit warmer. It was really funny the way everyone overestimated their strength and the wind and headed right for the center of the lake, then pooped out and barely made it back. I was honking like a goose when I finally made it back to shore.

I tore into another good book this evening—*Floods of Spring*. I've almost finished it and could hardly leave it to eat supper. It's about Missouri.

No more news.

What I Could Not Tell the Folks

We were ready to start the show we had been rehearsing for for more than a year. It was about time. We were sick and tired of rehearsals. We were especially fed up with having to go to London without the little swatch of blue cloth behind our silver wings that signified the wearer had flown combat missions. The B-17 pilots and the P-47 pilots had blue swatches. Silver wings without a blue swatch posed the question: If you are a pilot and you are not flying a bomber or a fighter in combat, what are you doing over here?

Practice intensified as winter turned into spring. We rendezvoused at night with other groups to form a long train of aircraft in formation, invisible from the ground. We towed CG-4A gliders, singly and in tandem. We towed the British Horsa glider, which could carry thirty infantrymen. We dropped British, Polish, and U.S. paratroopers. We pointed huge formations of troop-carrying aircraft at the English Channel as if we were an invasion spearhead destined for the French coast at Dieppe or Calais or Boulogne or Cherbourg. It was always a feint, designed to keep the Germans off balance. Once we reached the Channel, we would turn around and go home. Then on June 5, we did not turn around. We kept on going.

WATCHING THE WAR FROM A C-47

W e woke up one morning to discover the day had come. The whole base—including the village of Tadley—was sealed off. Barbed wire and armed guards penned us in. "Invasion stripes" had been painted on the wings of our airplanes and gliders. Three big white stripes and two blacks. (Overnight it seemed the zebra stripes had been painted on every Allied aircraft. There would be no mistaking foe for friend.)

The briefing room was papered with maps. On the maps were the routes, the landing zones, and the drop zones that were the war's most carefully guarded secrets. Now we were entrusted with those secrets. It was a huge thrill.

The "flak maps" were especially interesting. They showed, in red shading, where flak (antiaircraft fire) was expected to be heaviest.

We had great respect for German antiaircraft gunners. We imagined them all to be master sergeants, career guys weighed down with medals for marksmanship. Our high regard was based partly on an event that happened when the United States was first getting involved in the air war in Europe. We had sent a formation of B-26 medium bombers to attack the German torpedo-boat base at Ijmuiden in Holland. It was to be a low-level attack. Only one or two B-26s came back. After that encounter we did not send any more bombers on low-level missions against coastal targets. Now we were going to tow gliders into Normandy at five hundred feet and 110 mph. What should we expect? That was the question on everybody's mind.

NORMANDY

At about 11 P.M. on June 5 we were at our airplanes and gliders waiting for a 2 A.M. takeoff. Coffee-and-doughnut carts manned by the Salvation Army or the Red Cross circulated on the flight line. The music on a loudspeaker was "My Darlin' Nellie Gray."

Then, out of the woods around the airfield came the glider infantrymen, hundreds of them, faces blacked, bodies bristling with weapons. They moved in absolute silence. At a prearranged signal, this flood of soldiers divided into small groups and the groups advanced to their assigned gliders. There were no commands that I could hear, no sounds at all. It was a menacing display of disciplined stealth.

We took off, formed up, and headed for the Channel. The ceiling was low and there were raindrops on the windshield. The 74th Squadron was leading the formation, and our Group CO, Col. Bill Whitacre, was in the cockpit of the lead airplane with Capt. Alvin "Robby" Robinson, who, a month later, was chosen to be the personal pilot of Gen. Omar Bradley.

BAPTISM BY FIRE

Captain Robinson later described the approach to the Normandy coast. "We could see the Germans clearing their guns as the tracers went up into the air like the tails of rockets," he said. Robinson went on to describe the approach to the glider landing zone near Ste. Mère Eglise: "By now the shells were bursting all around us. Since we were the lead ship they didn't have our speed down and didn't realize we were making only 110 mph. I asked Mike in the glider [Col. Mike Murphy] how they were doing. He said they were getting the hell shot out of them." At the same time, Robinson's flight engineer reported on the interphone that the back end of their C-47 was getting badly hit. "I found out later," Robinson said, "that it was just concussions from the explosions that were making it sound like we were being hit."

I must have been a minute or two behind Robinson's aircraft. As he described, the concussions from exploding antiaircraft shells made near misses feel like hits. I was convinced that part of the nose of my C-47 had been shot away, and I expected to find extensive damage when it became light enough to see. But we came out of it virtually unscathed. A day or so later inspectors found a projectile—probably from a burp gun—lodged in one of the wheel wells of my C-47.

There was a moment, however, when I thought I was really in trouble. We had released our glider and were headed back over the Channel coast. Our altitude was down to one hundred or two hundred feet. Suddenly all I could see ahead and below were the hazy outlines of ships. We were barely clearing the superstructures of the larger ones. Then it hit me: This was the invasion fleet! They had every right to shoot us out of the sky. I was off the prescribed course and could have been assumed to be a German bomber. This is precisely what had happened during the airborne invasion of Sicily when the navy shot down some thirty C-47s. As it turned out, most of our aircraft passed directly over the fleet en route home. The navy knew who we were.

MY GLIDER PILOTS WEREN'T AS FORTUNATE

Pilot Bill Brown and his copilot Tommy Biggs, landing in the dark, collided with trees. Bill suffered a crushed foot, a knee injury, and a concussion. Biggs had compound fractures of both legs both above and below the knees. Their glider was carrying a signal officer, a noncom, and a radio jeep. The signal guys, unhurt, tried to extract the jeep from the wreckage, gave up, and left on foot. Later, two medics arrived and administered morphine to the glider pilots. That afternoon the medics hand-carried the glider pilots to a farmhouse that was a collecting point for the wounded where they spent the night. The next day they were transferred to a beach (probably Omaha) where they were picked up by a DUKW [an army amphibious landing craft that consisted of a 2½-ton GI truck fitted with ari-tight tanks (for bouyancy) and an outboard motor] and taken to a Landing Ship Tank (LST), which ferried them to England and a hospital in Oxford. (Brown and I got together in 2000 in the Officers' Club at Fort Bragg, North Carolina. That is when I finally learned what had happened to him on D-Day.)

GLIDER MISSION NO. 2 AND D-DAY FOLLOW-UP

We delivered gliders again on June 6, taking off from Aldermaston at about 4:30 P.M. I have a hazy recollection of being over the landing zone near Carentan in daylight. We may have made a third trip with gliders or paratroopers. I am not sure. As I remember, we were either flying, briefing, or debriefing for the better part of three days. I believe we were given Benzedrine or some stimulant to help us stay awake and alert. When there was a lull and we had time to sleep, we did not wake up for a long time. I remember thinking when I awoke that it was a weird time to be getting up.

Within a few days of D-Day we were landing on the Normandy Peninsula and evacuating wounded to British hospitals. John Devitt, a 73d Squadron flight leader, remembers that we had to thread our way through barrage balloon cables to reach the landing strip near Cherbourg. Bill Chaple, a 73d pilot, remembers that the strip was close enough to the fighting that he could distinguish the sound of the Germans' machine guns from that of the Americans.

We evacuated German wounded as well as American. I carried just two casualties on one trip. One was a GI, the other a German sniper. Both had head wounds but were ambulatory. Our flight engineer, George O'Sullivan, cradling a tommy gun, stationed himself between the wounded men for the duration of the flight.

GAS TO PATTON, MEDEVACS TO HOSPITAL

The Americans broke out of Normandy at Ste.-Lo. The breakout followed weeks of tough fighting in the hedgerows. The German army defending Brittany and western France was caught in an Allied pincers. In late July the pincers closed on the Germans in the vicinity of Falaise and Argentan. Allied fighter-bombers and artillery virtually destroyed the German divisions.

That allowed Gen. George Patton's Third Army to begin racing across France all the way to the Seine River, east of Paris. Patton's tanks would keep on rolling as long as they were fueled. But refueling became increasingly difficult as the tanks traveled farther away from the pipeline, which stopped at the Channel.

Getting gas to Patton's tanks then became our number one mission. We carried the fuel in five-gallon jerricans. We landed on grass strips that had been vacated by Germans—very recently, sometimes—and patched up by combat engineers. Unloading was done in a hurry by the whole crew. If a field hospital were nearby, we would fill the empty airplane with wounded soldiers, some on litters, some ambulatory. Then we would fly them home to Aldermaston, where they were moved to the military hospital in nearby Oxford.

On our flight line one morning we found four shiny four-engined aircraft, one for each squadron. They were B-24 bombers that had been modified to carry a large cargo of gasoline. Gone were the guns and gun turrets. Inside the fuselage, including what would have been the bomb bay, was a huge gas tank. The airplane, designated the C-109, had been designed as a tanker to deliver fuel over the Hump to the Chinese. I suppose some C-109s saw service in the CBI theater.

Our new C-109s had been delivered by Eighth Air Force bomber crews that had just finished their tours of combat duty. As I understood it, the B-24 crews were to remain with the airplanes long enough to transition a few of us into C-109 operation and maintenance. As I recall, the bomber crews delivered the airplanes and immediately disappeared. We had never handled four engines before. Most of us were unfamiliar with the C-109's tricycle landing gear, which required an approach to landing quite different from the one we used in our C-47 tail-draggers. (Tail-draggers was a term applied to aircraft that incoporated a tail wheel.)

For a few days we climbed in and around these shiny new birds like savages inspecting mirrors for the first time. Finally one of the squadron's senior pilots—Squadron Comdr. Terry Hutton, I believe it was— taxied to the runway, took off, circled the field a few times, and landed. That broke the ice. A number of us got "checked out" on the C-109 over the following weeks. I remember flying the C-109 as "instructor pilot" when I could not have had more than six hours' experience in the aircraft myself.

Later, Hugh Gunn flew the 73d's C-109 to France when our whole group moved there, and the big airplane remained parked beside the steel plank runway until the war in Europe was over. Our C-109 was never used to deliver fuel.

In the big scheme of things, the gasoline we delivered to Patton was only a tiny fraction of what he needed. No other fuel-delivery system available at the time proved adequate either, and the tanks had to come to a halt.

In my opinion—notwithstanding the inadequacy of our fuel delivery—it was when we were hauling supplies to the front and evacuating the wounded (and, later, the liberated POWs) that troop-carrier crews displayed the highest level of piloting skill, discipline, and resourcefulness. These missions brought into play everything we had learned in the pilot factory and afterward.

There was a new destination every day, usually a grass field in a newly liberated part of France or Belgium. Selection of the field was done by a team in some high-echelon headquarters. In the wee hours of the morning, the destination of the day and a delivery schedule were communicated to the squadrons at our base and at other troop-carrier fields in England. Takeoff times were staggered so squadrons would not create a traffic jam at the destination.

Still, traffic was usually heavy. To an approaching pilot, the field looked like a hive swarming with bees. There was no control tower, of course. On arrival, the leader of each squadron of eight to twelve airplanes maintained formation, circled the field, and waited his turn to lead his squadron into the landing pattern. Airplanes landed at intervals of ten-seconds or less, so the unloading area was always chock full of parked C-47s being emptied of jerricans and, sometimes, being loaded with casualties bound for a hospital in England.

These missions tested us on lessons we had been expected to learn in the pilot factory. Short-field landings and takeoffs, strange-field landings and takeoffs, dead-reckoning navigation, night formation (because sometimes we did not get home until after dark), weight-and-balance management—it all came into play.

The weather was another matter. We had learned to fly in an area where ceilings and visibility were often unlimited. Where we new flew—the British Isles, northern France, the Low Countries—the weather was often awful. An airfield could be socked in for days. Even when the winter sun came up bright and clear, you might have to spend half an hour sweeping frost off your wings.

Things could change fast. One late afternoon in the fall of 1944, we had four or five C-47s sitting on a muddy field in France. We had flight nurses on this trip, and we were ready to take on a full load of litter cases. The ceiling was low to begin with, and it looked like worse weather might be moving in. Before we loaded the evacuees, I decided to take off empty and circle the field to get a better look at what was coming. What I saw when we cleared the ground looked like the roll cloud in a classic cold front. It was down on the deck and closer than I had realized. I barely had time to do a 360 and skid to a stop at the upwind end of the field with one wheel in a slit trench. Then it was dark and raining buckets. We were able to load up and get out the next day.

HOLLAND (OPERATION MARKET-GARDEN)

The Allies had hoped to flank German defenses by attacking from Holland, driving into the Ruhr Valley and then on to Berlin. Some twenty thousand British and American airborne troops were to seize bridges over the Waal, Meuse, and Lower Rhine Rivers. This was to open the road to British armor, which would move north from Belgium across a comer of Holland and into Germany.

My squadron was involved with the 101st Airborne Division for two

Troop carrier air crews and glider pilots are addressed by Gen. Anthony McAuliffe of the 101st Airborne Division. This event took place at Aldermaston Air Base in the fall of 1944, just prior to the Allied airborne attack on Nazi forces in Holland. Air crews of the 73d and 74th squadrons are prominent in this photo. Photo courtesy of the 101st Airborne Association, Fort Campbell, Kentucky

days, starting on September 17, 1944. We dropped paratroopers the first day and towed gliders the second.

The first day went generally as planned. We flew up the highway where the British tanks were advancing, and we passed over the armored column at minimum altitude. As we continued north, the highway emptied and we crossed over what turned out to be a no-man's-land. Thereafter the tanks on the highway were German, and the tank crews, thinking we were bombers or fighter-bombers, scrambled to get their hatches closed and their weapons unlimbered. We ran into heavy fire from German gunners in the vicinity of the drop zone but made a good drop anyway.

Leaving the drop zone, I saw German antiaircraft fire from a patch of woods strike the three-ship element just ahead of me. One of the stricken C-47s started to go down as my element reached the German gun position. We were sitting ducks. At that instant, an RAF Mosquito appeared out of nowhere and dove on the German battery. The gun was silenced, and we passed over it unscathed.

On the second day, September 18, we towed gliders, and the weather was terrible. We may have had a five-hundred-foot ceiling at takeoff, but it kept closing down. Over the Channel the lowest layer of cloud more or less merged with the sea, and we had to go on top. The navigator Jim Taylor was in my plane, and Hugh Gunn and Bruce Phipps were piloting the other two airplanes in our element. We were flying at about twelve hundred feet, hoping to find a break in the cloud so we could descend to an altitude that would allow us to maintain visual contact with the ground.

Taylor, in the meantime, was navigating by time and distance. We knew where we were, relative to our intended course.

We were supposed to stay off the radio, but I began to hear plane-to-plane chatter. The pilots I heard talking could see where they were, it seemed to me. They were underneath the cloud layer that I was on top of. Taylor's calculations put us over the low, flat landscape in Belgium. I broke radio silence to tell Gunn and Phipps I was going to try a letdown through the undercast. I had decided that the risk was justified by the desperate situation on the ground in Holland. I told Gunn and Phipps that I would let them know when I was underneath and in the clear. I set the radar altimeter to signal "red" at fifty feet and began a slow descent.

I did not have radio contact with my glider pilot. He had no way of knowing what was going on. He had rudimentary flight instruments (airspeed, rate of climb, bank-and-turn indicator, and compass), but no training in blind flying. He was not supposed to be put in this position. He became disoriented as soon as he was enveloped in cloud. The glider, responding to the pilot's vertigo, pulled the tow plane into a crazy yaw. It was too late to try to get back on top. I kept descending, hoping to break into the clear in time for the glider pilot to regain control. Two things happened simultaneously: I saw through the windshield what appeared to be fence posts, and the warning light on the radar altimeter flashed red. I told John Matejka, the copilot, to release the tow rope, and we climbed out of the soup into the clear. We knew the glider and everyone and everything aboard was lost. Gunn and Phipps had disappeared. We headed back to Aldermaston.

I told the debriefing officer in detail what had happened. After debriefing I found out that Gunn and Phipps had wisely turned around and headed back to the Channel until they found breaks in the clouds that allowed them to release their gliders in the clear and in friendly territory. Later I discovered that other tow pilots that day had done what Gunn and Phipps did. I never talked about it again, and no one brought it up to me, nobody in my crew, not even my best friends, Smitty and Jack Miser. I believe they all could imagine the terror that must have filled that glider. They did not feel it necessary to remind me that my recklessness and bad judgment had caused the tragedy.

The glider pilot, I found out much later, had been new to the squadron. He was from Michigan. I do not know what his glider was carrying. I am still trying to forget that day.

BASTOGNE

Bastogne was the crossroads town in the Ardennes that became a key to the Allied victory in the Battle of the Bulge. German panzer divisions had bypassed Bastogne when they overran Allied positions in their surprise attack of December, 1944. But the town had to be taken because, in Allied hands, it was a threat to the German line of supply.

Bastogne was held by soldiers of the 101st Airborne Division. Their stubborn resistance was robbing the German attackers of the momentum they had initially achieved. But the 101st was running out of everything—ammunition, plasma, and food. The needed supplies were loaded onto troop-carrier airplanes in England. But nothing was flying. Bad weather effectively muzzled our fighter-bombers, which normally would have silenced the German artillery that was pounding Bastogne. Weather kept us on the ground, too.

Morning after morning we had breakfast at 4:00 A.M., a briefing at 5:00, and were in our airplanes around 6:00, listening for the start-engines signal. We would sit for hours some mornings, but the fog just hung in there. The Germans invited the 101st to surrender Bastogne, and General Anthony McAuliffe replied with his famous "Nuts!"

One day around Christmas the sun came out early and burned off the fog. We approached Bastogne flying at about three hundred feet on a course that took us over the lead tanks in the U.S. Third Army's relief column. Bastogne was just about three miles up the road from the U.S. tanks. The tank guys were waving. Our fighter-bombers were diving on German positions. We were delivering vital supplies. It was a thrilling experience. The fresh snow that covered everything made the whole scene appear deceptively benign.

ACROSS THE RHINE AT WESEL

In February, 1945, the 434th Troop Carrier Group, including my squadron, the 73d, moved from Aldermaston to a base in France at Mourmelon, a village near Rheims. We shared the base with the 101st Airborne, which had come to Mourmelon to rest and refit after Holland and—shortly after arriving—had been rushed by truck to Bastogne where the division distinguished itself again.

The facilities here had suffered a lot of wear and tear due to war or age or both. Our quarters were ramshackle compared with Aldermaston, and the airfield consisted of one steel plank runway and a control tower made of lumber and accessible only by a long ladder that had to be climbed hand over hand.

Here we resumed resupply flights to the front, often completing two trips in one day. Again, the destination was different every day, and on our return flights we sometimes carried POWs, newly liberated and deloused. John Devitt still has his passenger manifests from the POW flights. At the bottom of each manifest an officer in charge of the evacuation signed the following statement: "I certify that the individuals listed on this manifest have been disinfected and are authorized evacuation by air."

The POWs we carried were either U.S., French, or British. They had been marshaled by nationality into planeload groups of twenty-five. Their conditions varied. Most were gaunt but happy. An exception was a dour British soldier I talked with who had been captured when German parachutists and glider infantry seized the island of Crete in 1941. He was not looking forward to going back to England. Once I saw a tall and especially wretched-looking man in a strange uniform standing alone, observing the groups of twenty-five that were loading or waiting to be loaded. I was told that he was a Russian soldier.

We flew the French POWs to Le Bourget Airport in Paris, where each planeload, after disembarking, was loaded onto a stake bed truck, given bottles of wine, and driven down the Champs-Elysées to the cheers of Parisians. Most of these men had been POWs for almost five years.

The Rhine was crossed March 7 when the big bridge at Remagen was captured in an audacious action by troops of the U.S. 9th Armored Division. But the Allied Supreme Command had for some time planned to use its airborne army to breach the Rhine. The assault was titled Operation Varsity and was launched on March 24 from landing zones near Wesel, Germany. This was just across the river from the Dutch cities of Arnhem, Nijmegen, and Eindhoven, where the Allied airborne attack of September, 1944, had been defeated.

My group delivered paratroopers of the 17th Airborne Division. The sky was clear. I could look ahead and see that my squadron was part of a long train of airplanes that seemed to extend to the horizon. Then, looking to the right, I could see a parallel column of airplanes appear, heading in the opposite direction. These were airplanes that had released their gliders and dropped their paratroopers and were heading home. A number of these airplanes seemed to be on fire.

On the ground, Winston Churchill was watching the same thing. British Field Marshall Sir Bernard Montgomery had taken him to a spot on the west side of the Rhine where, through binoculars, he could see the attack occur. Churchill describes the scene in his *Memoirs of the Second World War:*

> It was full daylight before the intense roar and rumbling of
> swarms of aircraft stole upon us. After that in the course of half
> an hour over 2,000 aircraft streamed overhead in their forma-
> tions. The light was clear enough to enable one to see where the
> descent on the enemy took place. The aircraft faded from sight
> and then almost immediately returned toward us at a different
> level. . . . Soon one saw with a sense of tragedy aircraft in twos
> and threes coming back askew, asmoke or even in flames. It
> seemed however that nineteen out of twenty of every aircraft
> that had started came back in good order, having discharged
> their mission.

The mission was uneventful for me, my crew, and the rest of the squadron, as best I can recall.

REST LEAVE AT CANNES

I had already been to Paris, thanks to a lucky break. When GIs needed long underwear in the fall of 1944, the quickest way to deliver the longjohns was to fly them to Paris. That is how I got to the French capital while liberation fever was still running high. If things had gone as planned, I would have had to unload in Paris and return immediately to England. But taxiing out to takeoff, I ran over a K-ration tin that punctured my tail-wheel tire. A replacement tire was flown in, but not until the next day.

I got to Paris again in March, 1945, on a short "plum" assignment. It was not as pleasant as I had expected it to be. I was alone and did not understand what anybody was saying. The girls were still singing a German pop tune about "eine kleine Zigarette." Haven't they gotten the word? I wondered. I did manage to attend a show at Bal Tabarin, the fabulous nightspot. But I missed good old London and the English language.

Then in April, 1945, it was my turn to go on a one-week rest leave in Cannes on the French Riviera. Cannes was an official U.S. Army rest and relaxation "camp" for officers. Pretty much the same thing was reserved for enlisted men just up the coast in Nice.

My group, the 434th, could send two officers a week. My companion was Joe Leszcz, a pilot from the 74th Squadron. Joe and I must have been among the first in our group to get tickets to Cannes. We were flown to the little airport at Cannes where we were politely told to remove all insignia of rank. In Cannes we were not supposed to know a lieutenant from a colonel.

Rank would not have mattered anyway. From the time we arrived until we left, all we did was gape at the stunning beauty of Cannes. The little city was a sensory blast. Buildings exhibited a variety of pastel colors. Vines, trees, and flowers were in bloom. The sun was bright, the sea blue, the temperature balmy but not hot. Even the air seemed fragrant, sort of spicy.

Joe and I shared a room in the Carlton Hotel. Our room had a balcony that overlooked the palm trees on the Promenade, the beach, the blue Mediterranean. I had not known a place could be this gorgeous.

Joe and I rented kayaks, paddled to an island in the harbor, and discovered an old fort or castle. (The building was Fort Royal and the island was Sainte Marguerite, I later learned.) We were the only people on the island. The fort was an adventure, almost too good to be true. Doors were made of heavy old wood with strap hinges that creaked. Exploring what we assumed to be the fort's dungeon, I felt like I was the first person to venture into an Egyptian pyramid. We did not see the sign until we returned to where we had beached the kayaks. The sign said "VERBOTEN MINEN!"

Back at the Carlton we found out that the hotel staff should have warned us to stay off the island. The mines must have been cleared, though. We had walked all over the fort. If a mine had been there, we would have triggered it.

At the Carlton desk we signed up for dinner in the home of a Cannes family. The family we were assigned lived in a mansion on the boulevard. They were a well-to-do middle-aged couple with a young teenage son. They had invited the girl next door to join them for dinner, and she was a knockout. Before dinner, the *l'homme* of the house showed us headlines from newspapers that he had saved from the day that Lindbergh landed at Le Bourget. Lindberg was his hero. The dinner was spectacular, several courses and several kinds of wine. Afterward the son wheeled out a German motorcycle and we took turns riding it down the boulevard. Before we left, Joe and I both got the phone number of the girl next door, but I got to a phone first.

Camille (not her real name) seemed custom designed to inhabit this lovely place. She told me that what she liked to do in the summertime was hunt octopuses with a speargun. We walked out on a pier in the harbor in swimsuits, and she demonstrated how the speargun worked. She said she lived in the sea in the summer and skied in the Alps in the winter. I had never heard of a speargun and I had never met anyone, male or female, who knew how to ski. I had not known that the world she lived in even existed.

We went to the movie theater and saw Gary Cooper in *Lives of a Bengal Lancer*. Cooper was speaking dubbed-in French, but I knew that

Camille knew that Cooper was an American, and I hoped that some of his glamour would rub off on me. Someone in the row behind us tapped Camille on the shoulder. She stood up and faced the people behind us and motioned me to do the same. Practically all the people in the row behind us were on their feet. They were members of Camille's family and her friends. She introduced some of them, and we shook hands and resumed watching the movie. When it was over and we got up to leave, I noticed that most of the people who had been behind us had already gone. I wondered if they had been there more to chaperone than to see the movie.

There was a big dance at the Carlton the night before we were to leave Cannes, and Camille accepted my invitation. A large orchestra played the current Riviera favorite, an instrumental composition that had become, to me, the theme song for Cannes. It was called "Symphonie," and five or six years later it was exported to the States and became a fixture on our hit parade.

When I took Camille home, I was happy to see that the sky had changed from starry night to low cloud and fog. Joe and I were due to be picked up by a 434th airplane at the Cannes airport at 9 A.M. the next day. But I was absolutely sure that the airport would be closed due to weather, so I invited Camille to meet me for coffee on the Carlton terrace at 10:00 A.M. When I woke up the next morning, the clouds had gone, the sun was rising, and I knew with growing anguish that the airplane would be there at nine. I tried to get through to Camille on the phone. I tried at the hotel and again at the airport, but the operator and I did not understand each other. By ten I was almost back at my base, sick at heart.

About two months later I picked out a box of expensive bath soap at the Stix, Baer & Fuller department store in St. Louis. I remembered that good soap was a wartime luxury in France. I figured I owed Camille something for not showing up for coffee. I wanted her to know, too, that she had completely wowed me, for whatever that was worth. The box of soap sat on the screened porch at home for a month or so. One day it rained in on the porch and the box got soaked. We used the soap at home.

VE-DAY

I flew thirteen hours on VE-Day. John Devitt still has one of his passenger manifests from that day, May 8, which shows that he carried twenty-five newly liberated American POWs on one trip from Germany to either France or England. I would have been doing the same thing. Devitt and I probably made several trips each, judging by the number of hours I logged.

As the war was winding down, we flew deeper into Germany to pick up POWs. On one of those trips, I saw the first and only German fighter I would see in the air. It was also the first jet I had seen in action, one of Germany's new twin-jet ME-262s. We were at the same altitude, about a thousand feet above the ground. I was headed into Germany, and the jet pilot was hightailing it for France, presumably to surrender and find some sanctuary preferable to what he could expect in Germany. Just a few days before, on an airfield in Germany, we had seen several parked ME-262s that had apparently never been flown. We speculated that the jets were grounded because of lack of fuel or trained pilots.

We were flying every day over the part of France where the bloodiest battles of World War I had been fought. These battlefields had not caught my attention during the first few months that we were based in France. Now we often headed back to home base at Mourmelon in the late afternoon hours of April. The shadows were long and pronounced, the fields a uniform green in color. These conditions made it easy to make out thirty-year-old trench lines that undulated from horizon to horizon. Any question about the origin of these angular depressions in the natural curve of hill and pasture was answered by the names of nearby towns—Soissons, Château-Thierry, Metz, Verdun.

I was flying over these old trenches as the sun was setting on VE-Day. It looked like the Fourth of July. Tracers, flares, exploding shells, anything that would light up the sky was being fired. The war in Europe was over, and every GI who could get his hands on a weapon was celebrating.

At home base, the 101st Airborne had occupied the rickety control tower. Paratroopers were firing tracers from the tower, and I had to circle the field a time or two before a cease-fire was established and I was able to land.

HOME VIA THE SOUTHERN ROUTE

Going home did not mean going home to stay. We would get thirty-day leaves once we reached the States, then we would reassemble and fly to the Pacific for the invasion of Japan. That was our understanding of what lay ahead. When we got new airplanes for the trip home, that clinched it. We were headed for the Pacific by way of the States.

One question remained: Who would fly the twelve new planes of the 73d Squadron, and who would not? We had more pilots than we had airplanes, thanks to replacement pilots who had been fed into the squadron over the past year and a half. The word came down that the new planes should go to the best pilots, regardless of their total flying time and the length of time they had been with the squadron. The pilots not chosen would be redeployed to temporary locations in Europe. They would get home eventually, but it might take months.

This called for some tough decisions. The responsibility weighed heavily on Smitty, who had been promoted from operations officer to squadron commander. But I had been assistant operations officer under Smitty, and I became operations officer when he was elevated. That put me on the hot seat, too, in the matter of choosing who would fly home and who would redeploy.

The selection process left me frazzled. I was tired anyway. Smitty and I had been sharing ops officer duties. On one day he would lead the squadron to its designated destinations, and I would do the briefing, stay behind, coordinate with maintenance on aircraft availability for the next day, and arrange to have lunches on the flight line to expedite flying a second mission. The next day I would fly and Smitty would run the show on the ground.

I felt so used up by VE-Day that I assigned myself to fly home as co-pilot to my good friend Jack Miser. I may have done it to enable another pilot to fly home instead of being redeployed. Whatever my reason, it worked out well. The flight home was a restorative experience for me. I could look out the window at the fascinating sights below — Gibraltar, camel caravans, African jungle, Amazon jungle, and, finally, the coast-line of the southeastern United States. Jack did all the work.

Crossing the South Atlantic was a nine-stage trip in those days. We followed the route set up and managed by the air transport command (ATC). A few scenes still come to mind.

Mourmelon to Marrakech
We landed just before dark and were driven from the airfield through the city to ATC's quarters for transients. Two lasting memories: the blast of dry heat (a sharp contrast to northern France), and the high mud walls (six to eight feet) topped with shards of glass that surrounded houses in residential neighborhoods. We left the next day without having seen the Kasbah.

Marrakech to Dakar
Briefers at Marrakech warned us against going down for any reason in Ifni. Ifni is the stretch of desert between Morocco and Senegal now shown on some maps as Spanish Sahara. It was still called Ifni on our flight maps. The reason for not landing there, intentionally or otherwise, was that most of those who did so were never heard from again. I saw a few camels in Ifni but nothing else.

Dakar to Liberia
The desert gave way to jungle and occasional villages. Our destination airport was near a Firestone rubber plantation, I was told. Meals here were served in a huge open-sided shelter, with a thatched roof, on long trestle tables and benches. Behind each diner a Liberian native jogged in place. The jogging, I assumed, was to indicate the earnest-ness of the waiter to fetch refills or to clear plates. Bill Chaple, another 73d pilot, thought the waiters were boys because they were so small, but he was told they were male adults whose life span was only about thirty years.

Liberia to Ascension Island

Ascension was a big rock that stuck up out of the South Atlantic about halfway between Africa and South America. A runway had been built there to make the island a stepping-stone for intercontinental air traffic. We felt sorry for the people stationed there. There was nothing to do but fix box lunches for crews flying east or west. We got our box lunches and a briefing the morning after we landed. Next stop: the Western Hemisphere.

Ascension to Natal, Brazil

Natal was a major ATC base and quite uptown compared with the quarters that we had become used to. You had to wear a tie to eat in the officers' mess, and Jack Miser and I had just one tie between us. We cut the tie in two with a razor blade and fashioned two (sort of) bow ties that got us through the serving line. The next day we were driven to a stretch of empty beach where we bodysurfed for a few hours. What a treat!

Natal to Belem, Brazil

There was jungle all the way. Belem is at the mouth of the Amazon. We wanted to see this picturesque city but were not allowed to leave the base. (We were confined to base at all ATC fields, the one exception being the trip to the beach at Natal.) We watched from a distance a function at a church where the women wore long gowns and carried ornate parasols. It was most likely a wedding. It looked like a picture from the 1800s.

Belem to Georgetown, British Guiana (now Guyana)

We ran into a monster thunderstorm and experienced the worst-ever turbulence. It was probably unavoidable. The swimming pool at the base was an old, beautifully tiled pool like you would find at a country club. We played in the pool like kids.

Georgetown to Puerto Rico

Blue Caribbean below; romantic islands on all sides; I felt any remaining stresses melt away. The base (Borinquin) was beautiful, and for the first time in twenty months we had fresh milk to drink. I binged on milk.

The author's identification card, photographed and processed about July 5, 1945, the day he arrived at Hunter Field, Savannah, Georgia, following the end of the war in Europe.

Puerto Rico to Savannah, Georgia (Hunter Field)

We arrived on July 5, 1945. I called home first of all. Then I turned in my wristwatch, my .45, and other articles of equipment that belonged to the United States. I hated to part with the watch and found out, too late, that most guys had kept their watches. Jack and I told each other goodbye and caught our respective trains. We expected to see each other again in about thirty days.

EPILOGUE

My thirty-day leave was almost used up by August 6, the day Hiroshima was bombed. Three days later Nagasaki was destroyed. War did not end officially until September 2 with the signing of the surrender documents on the battleship *Missouri*, but there was a day shortly after Nagasaki and well before the official surrender when we knew the war was over. I was in the house with Mother and Dad and my sister Nancy when it sank in that I would not be going to the Pacific and that, in fact, the squadron that had been my wartime family would soon cease to exist. I wanted to sit down and think about it—about the good times and the bad times of the past three and a half years—and I went outside and sat down on the front steps by myself for about thirty minutes. I was sad for all the guys at Iwo Jima and Omaha Beach and in the B-17s over Germany who had not made it, like I had. I felt sad for everybody who would not come back. I felt lucky and very sad at the same time.

It was easy to feel lucky and even to see the war as the best thing that had ever happened to me. I had learned to fly, had logged eighteen hundred hours, and was being recruited by American Airlines. I had set foot in twenty-two foreign countries. I had gotten at least a glimpse of most of the major land battles that took place on the Western Front. Counting the portions of my paychecks that I had either sent home or invested in war bonds, the pay due me for deferred leave time, and the $500 bonus I got for every year of active duty I had served as a rated pilot, I was worth more than $5,000. By 1945 standards, I was a wealthy man when I turned twenty-four.

As soon as I was separated from the service, I took the train to Texas to visit my Uncle Tom and Aunt Jonnie, parents of Brooks, who had followed me into the air corps and who had been killed in Italy. Dad and I then drove up to South Dakota to hunt pheasants. We came back with fifty birds, dressed and frozen. Dad had manufactured binocular lenses for the navy during the war and was busy converting that plant to peacetime optical products. Also, he had just acquired dealerships for Evinrude outboard motors and Grumman canoes, and he wanted me to take over and build a business.

BACK TO CIVILIAN LIFE IN 1946

This was one of the few times that I openly disregarded Dad's wishes. I enrolled for the spring 1946 semester at the University of Missouri and graduated in 1948 with a Bachelor of Journalism degree. The degree came fast because I had done my freshman year in 1940–41 at the University of Oklahoma, and because I stayed for the summer semesters both years that I attended the University of Missouri. My first wife (we were married in 1947) had been an American literature major at the University of Colorado. She helped me stay resolved about finishing the journalism degree. We moved to Indiana when I was hired as a reporter by the *Evansville Press,* a Scripps-Howard paper with a circulation of fifty thousand.

After giving me a few months of general assignments, the management turned me loose to look for feature stories anywhere in the newspaper's sixteen-county circulation territory. I had the use of the company car and a Speed Graphic camera. The job was a plum for a cub like me, fresh out of J-school. The pay, though, was Third World. I started at $200 a month. Three raises added a total of $18.50 to my paycheck. When I had an opportunity to join the Air Force Reserve Wing in Columbus, Indiana, I took it—not because I wanted to fly, but simply because I would get paid for going on duty one weekend or so per month.

BACK TO THE MILITARY IN 1951

It was May, 1951, when I signed up. President Truman had just relieved General MacArthur as our man in charge of operations in Korea. A week later the Indiana wing was called to active duty. I could have opted out, but I committed to a two-year tour. Financially, at least, it made sense. As an air force major with flight pay, my paycheck would be more than three times what it had been on the newspaper—all the more important now that there was a baby in the picture, the first of five.

Returning to military life was like attending a reunion. All the pilots in the organization had flown in World War II. They had experienced a variety of aircraft and combat theaters. Capt. Joe Pound, a wonderful guy who became my close friend, had flown the Hump from India to China in a C-47 named *My Assam Dragon.* Another pilot had bailed out over Tibet and spent months sheltered and then guided by natives to his eventual rescue. Another had been flying cargo and passengers over the Andes in South America for a commercial air service ever since World War II. We were a pool of experienced pilots that the air force reached into to fill vacancies in Korea. Joe Pound went to Korea as an A-26 pilot after transition at Perrin Field in Texas. Walter "Doc" Savage went to Korea to fly F-86s. Those of us who stayed true to our two-years-only pledge did not have to worry about being shipped out.

Our wing commander was Gen. Lacey V. Murrow, the brother of Edward R. Murrow. That was a significant plus to me, dedicated as I was to anything related to journalism. The wing was the same old 434th tactical group that I had belonged to in the Army Air Corps of World War II, but it was now beefed up logistically and administratively so that it could operate independently in the new air force scheme of things. We still flew trucks, only now they were C-46s instead of C-47s. The Curtis C-46 had more power and cargo capacity than the C-47, but it lacked the responsiveness of the older airplane. It was one of the last of the tail-draggers. The pilot of a C-46 in landing configuration sat higher above the runway than he did in any other aircraft in the inventory. I wound up logging four hundred hours in the C-46, bringing my total hours to twenty-two hundred.

When I reported to General Murrow (and he pointed out to me that my collar insignia were pinned on backward) all the good positions in the tactical group (the slots for flying officers) had already been filled. Reservists in this wing had been flying together for a long time. I was assigned to wing operations with the title of liaison officer. It was a nothing job. My counterpart was a paratroop major from the 17th Airborne Division. Most of the time we could be found in the gym playing volleyball.

Late in 1951 the wing moved from Indiana to Lawson Field at Fort Benning, Georgia. There we established a school designed to refurbish the flying skills of pilots who had been stuck in desk jobs since the end of World War II. "Retread" students came from bases all over, including the Pentagon. Each student got sixty hours of familiarization in a C-46 and a course in survival taught by Army Rangers. Then the student was sent to Korea as a replacement pilot. The school was run very efficiently by one of the 434th's pilots, Capt. John Bassett.

As wing liaison officer, I was also a sort of second assistant wing operations officer. Over a period of several months, the operations officers above me were reassigned. One went to the Army War College, another to the Command and Staff School. All of a sudden I was *the* acting wing operations officer, responsible for forty-eight C-46s and crews. At about the same time, the wing was notified that a big practice maneuver was coming up. Ours would be one of three wings involved, which together marshalled a total of about 130 aircraft. We would drop the paratroopers of the 82d Airborne Division. Our wing would have operational control, which meant that I would be the briefing officer.

The briefing took place in the main theater at Fort Bragg, North Carolina. I was scared stiff. From where I stood on the stage, manning my overhead projector, it looked as though every officer sitting in the first row was a general. I got through it. The drop came off okay, too, after a short weather delay. That night I flew back to find a four-hundred-foot ceiling at Lawson Field. The instrument letdown procedure at Lawson utilized a beacon. I had probably practiced the procedure but I had never used it out of necessity. Sitting beside me in the right seat was the wing flight inspector. He was, in effect, the chief pilot of the wing. His main job was to keep pilot proficiency at an acceptable level. I am sure he talked me through the letdown procedure. Anyway, it went well. I remember feeling more proud of that letdown than I was of having briefed the 82d Airborne.

I started looking for a civilian job a month or so before my two-year tour ended in June, 1953.

BACK TO CIVILIAN LIFE IN 1953

I could have returned to the *Evansville Press* or accepted offers from other Scripps-Howard papers. A magazine job sounded better, though. I wrote to an aviation publication in Dallas called *Flight*. The publisher responded that he did not need a writer; but he knew that TEMCO Aircraft Corporation in Dallas was looking for one. The job was in TEMCO's public relations department, and I took it.

The new company occupied half of the giant North American Aviation plant that had employed fifty thousand aircraft builders during the war. Robert McCullough had headed the plant during the war. When the war ended, McCullough gambled that he and a select group of his best production people could win enough subcontracts to stay in business. He was right. All of aviation's prime contractors wanted TEMCO as a subcontractor. As the Cold War took shape, TEMCO built major sections of aircraft for Boeing, Martin, McDonnell, Lockheed, and others. As TEMCO's public relations writer, I learned the lingo of the assembly line, machine shop, flight test, quality control, and contract administration.

At lunch one day with the account executive from TEMCO's ad agency, I was told that I was wasting my time. You ought to be with an ad agency, the executive said. There were some good ones in Dallas, and coincidentally, the biggest and best of the Dallas agencies was looking for a writer with aviation experience. I was hired and began what turned out to be a forty-year career as an ad-man.

Aviation experience was the key I used to get into the "idea business," which was going strong at good ad agencies during the 1960s and 1970s. I wrote ads and marketing strategies for Vought, Bell Helicopter, Aerospatiale, Mooney, American Airlines, Frontier Airlines, and Philippine Airlines. I also wrote for IBM, Texas Instruments, Frito-Lay, Borden's Milk, Pearl Beer, and other non-aviation companies. But I almost always had a client in aviation. When I was seventy and ready to quit the nine-to-five routine, some of the last work I did was for Turbomeca, the French manufacturer of jet engines.

BACK TO THE PILOT FACTORY: AN APPRAISAL

As one of some two hundred thousand young men who entered the pilot factory as raw material and came out somewhat finished products, what did I think of the process? There was no time for contemplation then. There is now.

I saw a bunch of absolute dodos like me converted into disciplined military aviators—junior birdmen, of course, but dedicated to increasing their proficiency. I did not see or hear of a single serious accident in any phase of my cadet training. Apparently, my contingent was lucky in that respect. "As cadets progressed through the three stages of flight training," historian Rebecca Cameron observes, "the enterprise grew more deadly. . . . Few airmen in basic escaped seeing or knowing somebody who died in a training accident." Cameron maintains that statistics demonstrate that flying, "even in the benign early stages, was a highly dangerous occupation." The danger may have been the result of the air corps' wartime speedup (by three to four months) of the conventional pilot-training program, or the lowering of qualifying requirements—or Cameron's observations apply to earlier days when trainer aircraft were themselves more dangerous. In any case, it is hard to find a concern about danger in my letters. As cadets, we were definitely aware of the importance of flying safety. That was something that was drummed into us from the start. Fear of crashing, I believe, was somewhat remote, not like the fear of washing out, which was always present.

One of the training establishment's biggest responsibilities to the cadet came last in the training cycle; it was that of fitting the graduate pilot into the operational slot most appropriate for him. Should he pilot a fighter, a heavy bomber, or a medium bomber? Should he be an instructor, a transport pilot, or a ferry pilot? The decision was subjective (based largely, and I believe correctly, on flight instructor input). It was also influenced by the current or projected need for particularly qualified pilots (fighter, bomber, etc.) in the various combat theaters and by the number of replacement pilots in the pipeline.

I did not get what I wanted, which was fighters. Even worse was what I *did* get: C-47s, "Gooneybirds."

Looking back at what I had to offer, I believe the air corps made a wise decision. I was a slow learner. Give me a new airplane to fly and eventually I would figure it out, but in 1942 we had to learn quickly: the penalty for mistakes was quite high, and I made quite a few mistakes. I probably needed a forgiving airplane. That is not to say that all pilots assigned to C-47s needed forgiving airplanes. Many of those with whom I served were more than just competent C-47 fliers. I believe they would have performed well in any World War II aircraft. The circumstance that put us in C-47s most likely was the looming need for transport pilots.

Why did I not keep on flying? There were other things I wanted to do. Once in the 1970s I decided it was stupid of me to let my flying experience atrophy. I picked out a flying school at Love Field in Dallas and started studying for the written exam I would have to pass in order to get a private license. My plan was to rent planes and take trips. I scheduled a flying lesson while I studied for the written exam. The instructor and I agreed on a time and place to meet, but the instructor did not show up. When I called him at home, he said the ceiling or the visibility was below minimum. He implied that I should have known that just by looking at the sky. The weather had looked fine to me—the 434th would have flown a fifty-ship formation on a day like that. I lost interest at that point.

Conclusion? For me, the pilot factory and everything it led to was a great adventure. I was fortunate in many ways. I could have been assigned to fly an Eighth Air Force B-17 when the crews of those heavy bombers were suffering appalling losses over France and Germany. Instead, in a Troop Carrier C-47, I had what amounted to a general officer's view of some of the most crucial military contests that took place in the European theater. I was lucky, too, in that my mission assignments did not require me to operate from the same old runway day after day. We troop-carrier pilots flew into and out of airstrips all over France, Belgium, and Germany. We saw everything up close—refugees, wounded GIs, German prisoners, and newly liberated villages.

There were sad times for sure. Saying goodbye to close friends was always tough for me, and there was a lot of that. The death of my cousin Brooks when his plane crashed in Italy did not hit me hard until well after the war when his remains were brought home to Dallas for a memorial service. Those sadnesses are now long gone.

My mother, who saved my letters, lived to celebrate her hundredth birthday, surrounded by grandchildren and great-grandchildren.

Dad died in 1956 but was here long enough to move his optical-manufacturing business to Waynesville, Missouri, where he became something of a local celeb.

My sister Nancy is married to Vice Adm. Jon Boyes, who was (among many other things) skipper of the revolutionary nuclear submarine called *Albacore*. They live in Hot Springs Village, Arkansas. (Jon Boyes died unexpectedly on September 21, 2004.)

My cousin Bud (Reuben Gentry, the B-26 driver), and his wife Harriet live in Mesa, Arizona, where Bud was a docent at the Champlin Fighter Museum for many years and Harriet ran the gift shop.

John Devitt, Hugh Gunn, Jack Miser, Fred Jones, Boris Shvetzoff, and I still keep in touch.

Bill Brown, my D-Day glider pilot, lives in Fort Walton Beach, Florida. I hope to see Bill and his son Robert again soon.

Smitty, Li'l Dog Pierce, and other close friends from those years are gone. But I will always remember our days together, thanks to the letters mother saved.

NOTES

CHAPTER 3

1. Wesley Frank Craven and James Lee Cate, *The Army Air Forces in World War II*, vol. 1, 115–16.
2. Asher Lee, *The German Air Force*, 30.
3. British Air Ministry, *The Rise and Fall of the German Air Force, 1933–1945*, 28.
4. Ibid., 33, 41.
5. Ikuhiko Hata and Yasuho Izawa, *Japanese Naval Aces and Fighter Units in World War II*, 409, 417.
6. British Air Ministry, *Rise and Fall of the German Air Force*, 13–15.
7. Hata and Izawa, *Japanese Naval Aces*, 426–27.
8. Ibid., 355.
9. British Air Ministry, *Rise and Fall of the German Air Force*, 41.
10. Craven and Cate, *Army Air Forces*, 1: 116.
11. Craven and Cate, *Army Air Forces*, 6: 558.
12. Ibid., 456–58.
13. Rebecca Cameron, *Training to Fly: Military Flight Training, 1907–1945*, 384.
14. Craven and Cate, *Army Air Forces*, 6: 440–43.
15. Cameron, *Training to Fly*, 388.

SOURCES

Alexander, Thomas E. *The Stars Were Big and Bright: The United States Army Air Forces and Texas during World War II*. Austin: Eakin Press, 2000.

Arnold, H. H. *Global Mission*. New York: Harper Brothers, 1949.

British Air Ministry. *The Rise and Fall of the German Air Force, 1933–1945*. London: Her Majesty's Stationery Office, 1983.

Cameron, Rebecca. *Training to Fly: Military Flight Training, 1907–1945*. Washington, D.C.: Air Force History and Museums Program, 1999.

Craven, Wesley Frank, and James Lee Cate. *The Army Air Forces in World War II*. Vols. 1 and 6. Chicago: University of Chicago Press, 1955.

Faber, Harold. *Luftwaffe: A History*. New York: Times Books, 1977.

Fletcher, Eugene. *Mister: The Training of an Aviation Cadet in World War II*. Seattle: University of Washington Press, 1992.

Form One. Classbook of Class 42–J. Randolph Field, Tex: Aviation Cadet Club, 1942.

Hata, Ikuhiko, and Yasuho Izawa. *Japanese Naval Aces and Fighter Units in World War II*. Translated by Don Cyril Gorham. Annapolis, Md.: Naval Institute Press, 1989.

Irving, David. *The Rise and Fall of the Luftwaffe: The Life of Field Marshal Erhard Milch*. New York: Little, Brown, 1973.

Lee, Asher. *The German Air Force*. London: Duckworth, 1946.

Maupin, Robert N. *Flying Cadets of World War II: They Delivered the Bullets and Bombs that Ultimately Spelled—Victory!* New York: McGraw-Hill, 1999.

Mitcham, Samuel W. *Men of the Luftwaffe*. Novato, Calif.: Presidio, 1988.

Severe, Errol D. *The Last of a Breed*. Eureka Springs, Ark.: Lighthouse Productions, 1997.

Slipstream. Classbook of Class 42–J. Garner Army Air Field, Tex.: Class of 42-J, 1942.

Texas State Historical Association. "Garner Army Air Field." In *The Handbook of Texas Online.* http://www.tsha.utexas.edu/handbook/online.

Young, Charles H. *Into the Valley: The Untold Story of USAAF Troop Carrier in World War II, from North Africa through Europe.* Dallas: PrintComm, 1995.

INDEX